A TRAIN THROUGH TIME

A TRAIN THROUGH TIME

A Life, Real and Imagined

Elizabeth Farnsworth

With Photo Art by Mark Serr

COUNTERPOINT

BERKELEY

Library of Congress Cataloging-in-Publication Data is available.
ISBN 978-1-61902-843-2

Cover design by Gopa & Ted2, Inc.
Interior design by Megan Jones Design

COUNTERPOINT
2560 Ninth Street, Suite 318
Berkeley, CA 94710
www.counterpointpress.com

Printed in the United States of America
Distributed by Publishers Group West

10 9 8 7 6 5 4 3 2 1

For my husband, Charles Farnsworth, and our family
Jenny and Chris Fellows
Colter, Monique and Heath

Sam Farnsworth and Charlotte Hamilton
Gilbert, Daisy and Thomas

What is a self when riding along
clackety-clack, in the rain—?
(Grieving intensity, it is a fire egg . . .
A wishbone cave in a book on the history of flame.)

—From Brenda Hillman's
"A Halting Probability, on a Train"
(From *Seasonal Works with Letters on Fire*)

Portland Rose-Gold Coast 17-23 Example	Streamliner City of St. Louis-San Francisco Overland 9-27 ▲ Example	Table E Condensed Schedules All Trains Daily	San O Stre City E
		Wabash	
11.40 SUN	4.00 SUN	Lv St. Louis (C.S.T.) .... Mo. Ar	12
7.25 MON	9.00 SUN	Ar Kansas City.................. " Lv	7
8.30 MON	9.30 SUN	Lv Kansas City Union Pacific .. Mo. Ar	
✶	✶	" Lawrence...................Kan. Lv	
9.38 "	10.37 "	" Topeka.......................... " "	
10.33 "	11.30 "	" Manhattan...................... " "	
11.02 "	11.58 SUN	" Junction City.................. " "	
✶	✶ MON	" Abilene........................ " "	
11.54 "	12.40 "	" Salina.......................... " "	
1.36 "	2.23 "	" Hays........................... " "	
2.05 "	3.00 "	Ar Ellis (C.S.T.).................. " Lv	
1.14 "	2.09 "	Lv Ellis (M.S.T.).................. " Ar	
2.24 "	3.20 "	" Oakley.........................	
3.14 "	4.09 "	" Sharon Spr.....................	
5.09 "	6.07 "	" Limon.........................	
7.00 "	7.59 "	Ar Denver........................	
7.30 "	8.25 "	" Denver........................	

PART I

S EVERAL YEARS AGO, at Skywalker Ranch in northern California, the child I used to be appeared out of nowhere and asked a haunting question that I couldn't answer and can't forget.

It happened in the Technical Building among old movie posters and other treasures from George Lucas's collection. I was overseeing the audio mix of a documentary film I had codirected. We had already labored for three ten-hour days, and I was tired and worried that we'd miss the deadline for the San Francisco Film Festival. Editor Blair Gershkow and sound mixer Pete Horner were making most of the decisions. I didn't trust my judgment anymore.

Pete cleaned up the audio of an exhumation on a farm in southern Chile. I heard grains of dirt shaken through a sieve. On screen, Judge Juan Guzmán, the subject of the film, watched as a forensic anthropologist looked for pieces of bone and other evidence of violent murder thirty years earlier.

She picked something small and dirty out of the sieve and exclaimed, "*Mira!* Look! It's part of a cheekbone."

Guzmán said, "Could you pass it to me?"

"It's the lower part of the bone."

"So the cranium must be here?"

"Yes, these are human remains."

The judge held the bone gently in his hand. In 1973 he had toasted General Augusto Pinochet's bloody coup with champagne. Now he was investigating Pinochet's crimes.

A door opened nearby, and I heard laughter. They were mixing a comedy.

Lucky them.

Pete replayed the exhumation scene over and over, sweetening the sound.

I bolted from the dark room and ran down the stairs, past a poster for *Paths of Glory,* to a large atrium where a copper-colored man stood among ficus and ferns. I had seen him many times before and knew who he was, but now he stood in a pool of radiance streaming from the skylight above, which caught my eye. I stopped to look at him more closely.

He was about three feet tall and had a fat belly, big mustache, and eyes the color of emeralds. He was Tik-tok, Dorothy Gale's mechanical friend from Walter Murch's 1985 film *Return to Oz.*

I heard the voice of Judge Guzmán: "So the cranium is here?" I must have left the mixing room door open.

Stepping over a protective barrier and brushing plants aside, I kneeled in front of Tik-tok and hugged him. Then, time did something I can't explain. I felt a jolt, like electricity, and saw myself as the girl who had loved the Oz books half a century before.

That girl asked, "What sent you on a path through death and destruction?"

Minutes passed. Memories flashed through my mind like film in a projector.

A green snake, thin as a pencil, rising from an altar in Cambodia.

A plain wooden file drawer with 3 x 5 cards for each of the *desaparecidos* in Chile. Randomly, I take out a card and read the name—Jorge Müller, a friend.

A man on a bridge across the Euphrates, haloed by the setting sun.

We finished the mix at Skywalker Ranch, and *The Judge and the General* screened successfully in festivals and on public television. After that, still haunted by the child's question, I began to fit memories together, like bones from an exhumation.

TOPEKA — WINTER 1953

I woke up in the dark that morning as the whooshing sound drew near and prayed that whatever it was would stay outside.

I had seen it once—a dark shape hovering above the bed, bellowing—*whooooshhh whooooshhh*. When I told Mother, she called it the "monkey with a motor on its tail."

"Nothing to fear," she said.

I tried to call for help, but fright stole my voice away.

Suddenly—the ring of an alarm clock, and I was saved, at least on this morning. My father came in the room. "It's time, Elizabeth. Today's the day."

I dressed in new blue jeans, grabbed my overnight bag and teddy bear, and waited at the top of the stairs. I had recently turned nine. My sister, Marcia, who was fifteen, and our dog, Cindy, had gone to an aunt's house, where they would stay while my father and I were away.

I waited for several minutes before looking into my parents' bedroom to see why Daddy hadn't come. He stood in front of Mother's dresser, staring at her hand mirror as if he'd never seen it before. Then he packed it under a sweater in his suitcase and turned and saw me waiting.

I could tell he didn't want to leave. I couldn't wait to go.

Outside, an icy wind almost knocked me down. My grandfather had arrived early—a familiar trait in our railroad family—to take us to the station. We drove across the flatness of Topeka, weaving through neighborhoods so dark that I could hardly see the houses, passed my sister's high school with its brightly lit tower, and crossed the river on the Kansas Avenue Bridge. I waited for my father to tell a story about these places—he liked history—but neither he nor my grandfather spoke.

At the Union Pacific Station, our train, the Portland Rose, was late, and I sat on a wooden bench in the huge waiting room, watching people walk up and down, their voices echoing off the high walls. Somewhere down the track, a steam engine was switching cars—*whoosh, whoosh, whoosh.* The labored breathing sounded like the monster at home in the night.

A gust of wind shook windows behind me, and then— the deep rumble of a diesel engine. We walked outside and watched as it approached, brakes squealing, headlight probing the dark.

This train will take us to another world—like Dorothy's tornado I thought.

A porter took our bags and showed us to our bedroom, which he called a compartment. He had made up the berths so we could go back to sleep. It was five o'clock in the morning.

As we pulled out of Topeka, my father said, "The locomotive has the power of more than a thousand horses."

I imagined them pulling us across the prairie, my beloved home.

CAMBODIA—1993

I take in the smells of Phnom Penh as we drive through dark streets—wood fires, river, rotting fish. We're headed for a military base just outside of town, where we'll catch an early-morning ride to Banteay Meanchey, a province bordering Thailand in the north. The helicopter, a Russian Mi-17, painted white with "UN" in black letters on both sides, is warming up on the tarmac when we arrive. We'll leave at first light.

I'm excited about the trip but keep flashing back in my mind to Topeka (sorrel horse, hedge apples along a fence line), which means I'm more nervous than I thought.

Remnants of the Khmer Rouge still control some places we're going. The group's leaders signed a peace agreement and cooperated at first in the run-up to UN-sponsored elections, but now they're trying to stop the vote. This is the largest UN nation-building operation to date, and many countries have contributed troops and equipment, including the chopper. But no head of state wants to take losses, so UN soldiers have been ordered to avoid confrontations with any of the warring parties, including Khmer Rouge guerrillas.

Cambodia feels different than when we were here for *The NewsHour* two years ago. Hope lies heavy around us like the pre-monsoon air.

We board the helicopter, and the Russian pilot takes off toward the rising sun, banks north and a little west, and crosses the junction of the Tonle Sap and Mekong Rivers, which are flowing slowly in these last weeks before monsoon rains begin. In the dim light, I can barely see the great lake fed by the Tonle Sap River, which now flows southeast but will reverse direction when the drenched Mekong backs up.

As the sun rises higher, I see jungle, water, and occa-sional towns. Then the pilot noses down the copter, and the towers of Angkor Wat shimmer in the early light. No one speaks as we circle. Someone cowers in a courtyard below. After three ever-wider passes, we fly northwest again. The pilot points to another helicopter, a white Mi-17, lying wrecked on the ground.

"Was it shot down?" I can't decipher his answer over the engine's noise.

A platoon of Dutch marines is waiting for us in Banteay Meanchey. They load cameraman John Knoop, soundman Jaime Kibben, an interpreter, and me into a Land Rover with a mounted, manned machine gun behind the driver. The marines form a three-vehicle convoy with us in the middle, and we drive northwest on a dirt road that has been mined by one of the competing Cambodian factions. John points to sandbags under our feet with a wry smile and begins to film. We head for villages where Khmer Rouge soldiers have threatened to kill anyone who votes in the elections for a constituent assembly, now two weeks away.

Thirty-six UN employees in Cambodia have died as a result of hostile actions.

After about an hour, the convoy stops, and we walk single file down a narrow path to a cliff overlooking a deep and verdant valley, a place where the competing Cambodian factions have not yet denuded a large forest. Using binoculars, the soldiers check for signs of cutting, because the UN has placed an embargo on timber exports to block a source of income for the warring groups. In this place, at least, a green canopy stretches for miles before us, undisturbed in the hot, midday light.

On the way back to rejoin the convoy, a sergeant warns us again to stay on the narrow path; the surrounding area has been mined—by whom he doesn't say. We stop to reconnoiter an open-air temple—a thatched roof sheltering a large statue of Buddha surrounded by unlit candles. In the shadow of the Buddha, a snake hisses and uncoils, rising thin and scaly green. None of us knows what kind of snake it is. A sergeant steps between me and the snake, and I nod my thanks.

The memory repeats like a stuck tape. The snake rises. The Dutch sergeant moves to my side. Again and again.

The convoy travels farther along the mined road and then turns toward one of the threatened villages. We pass huts and a warehouse where Khmer Rouge soldiers in ragged uniforms are loading bags of rice onto a truck. Are they stealing it? One raises his Kalashnikov and aims it at

our car. He looks about sixteen. As we pass, he lowers the weapon and laughs.

On another day, we film a UN volunteer from Milwaukee, tall and stately with freckles and straw-colored hair, teaching peasants how to mark a ballot and assuring them that the Khmer Rouge are lying. "No satellite in the sky will be able to reveal how a person votes," she tells them.

"If the village chief tells you to vote for this or that party, you say, 'No, it's my choice.' A human right is something all of us are born with. No one can give or take it away. It's yours from the time you are born."

The villagers squatting before the makeshift stage are illiterate. Few have ever held a pencil. Some look weak from hunger. Does the volunteer note the chasm between her experience and theirs? It would be easy to mock her, but I am surprised to feel moved, even hopeful. I admire her courage and the UN's determination to press forward with elections in spite of threats from the Khmer Rouge.

"Thomas Jefferson meets Pol Pot," a reporter from *The Guardian* says later over dinner. "Bloody fine show if you ask me."

WHEN LIGHT SEEPED around the window shade that first morning on the train, I climbed down the ladder and looked outside. Wind blew sleet hard against the glass. The *clickety-clack* of the wheels on the track reminded me of a metronome keeping time. Looking around, I saw that my upper berth could be folded into the wall, and my father's bed would make a seat big enough for two. There was a chair in the corner. I liked the way everything fit *just so*— like a playhouse. Even the sink could be stowed. My father watched, smiling, from his berth.

He wanted me to love trains like he did.

His father had left high school to lay track for the Santa Fe and was now an executive with that railroad, but we were traveling on the Union Pacific to experience the northern route to San Francisco. My father liked dramatic weather, and the year before we had watched news reports about a train stuck in a blizzard in the mountains of California. "Maybe it will happen to us," he'd teased before we left home.

Sitting next to him on the bed, I held Louie up to the window to see cows and horses in fields along the tracks. He was a small brown bear whose fur had worn thin from years of hugging. Next to me were Mother's hand mirror, my new Toni doll, and a book, *The Road to Oz.*

I wanted them close when so much was changing.

Before reading to Louie, I described what he'd missed in the story so far. The orphan Dorothy Gale had wandered away from the farm in Kansas where she lived with her aunt and uncle and gotten lost "somewhere near to Oz." Now she and her companions were walking down an enchanted road toward the Emerald City in search of a princess with the power to send them home.

I read aloud, "Turning the bend in the road, there came advancing slowly toward them a funny round man made of burnished copper, gleaming brightly in the sun. Perched on the copper man's shoulder sat a yellow hen, with fluffy feathers and a pearl necklace around her throat.

"'Oh Tik-tok,' cried Dorothy, running forward. When she came to him the copper man lifted the little girl in his copper arms and kissed her cheek with his copper lips. . . . 'This,' turning to her traveling companions, 'is Mr. Tik-tok, who works by machinery, 'cause his thoughts wind up, and his talk winds up, and his action winds up—like a clock.'"

My father called Tik-tok a robot or automaton, but I thought of him more like a child who couldn't always do what adults expected of him.

Later we walked forward through the train to the dining car, where tables were covered with white linen and waiters called stewards wore spotless white coats. As we sat down, I noticed a girl about my age across the aisle with her mother and father. They were writing on a pad like the ones my friends and I used when playing waitress at home. My father explained that on the train, we filled out our order and a steward picked it up. In the past I would have wanted to make friends with the girl, but now I feared she'd ask questions.

When she finished her pancakes, she came across the aisle and sat down at our table without waiting to be invited.

She spoke directly to me. "I'm Sally from Tulip Lane in St. Louis, and those are my parents. I'm ten years old. Who are you?"

Daddy waited for me to answer, and when I didn't, he said, "I'm Bernerd, and this is Elizabeth, who just turned nine. We're on our way to California for a vacation."

The girl wore a plaid skirt, white blouse, and patent leather shoes and seemed older than ten. Her hair was blonde with stylish bangs; mine was light brown and held back on each side of my face by plastic barrettes.

I bet she's in fifth grade, I thought. I was in fourth.

She asked, "Why are you going to California? Do you have a dog?"

I wanted to say something but couldn't. I didn't know for sure why we were traveling to California and was trying to avoid thinking about Cindy, our dog, who I feared would be left alone at my aunt's house. I knew how it felt to be too long alone.

I wished the girl would go away. I didn't want a friend on the train.

"Let's go exploring," she said, jumping up from the table. Assuming I'd follow, she walked past the galley, the train's kitchen, and down the passageway until I couldn't see her anymore.

I stayed where I was, finishing my French toast.

A few minutes later, the door at the end of the car opened and closed, and then opened and closed again. I heard the sighing noise, like an intake of breath. My father had explained that pneumatic doors between the passenger cars of a train were controlled by compressed air.

"That's why they sound like they're breathing," he said.

The door down the corridor opened again. At least Sally from St. Louis was curious. I liked that.

Daddy excused me to join her. Together, we opened the door and watched it wheeze shut. Then we did it again. We were standing in the vestibule between the cars. Sally pointed down at the narrow space between us and the next car. Snow-covered prairie and wooden ties raced by under our feet. I heard the deep horn of the engine warning horses and cows off the track.

"Do you think trains can go faster than time?" I asked Sally. "Will we arrive in California and no time will have passed?"

"What do you mean?"

"Because we're traveling so fast, won't we get ahead of where we'd be if we'd stayed home?"

"I don't know," she said. "I never thought of that before."

TOPEKA — 1949

April. The smell of hyacinths filled the air. I glanced out an open window of my Randolph School classroom and saw my mother walking up a path flanked by crabapple trees in bloom.

A thunderstorm during the night had left rivulets of water flowing to a nearby creek, and she skipped over them like a child.

When she came into the room, I jumped up, surprised, because she had never picked me up so early before. She stood in the front of the room and whispered to Miss Gray, who beckoned me to come forward. Mother took my hand

and we left. Outside, white blossoms swirled as we ran down the path.

I asked where we were going.

"We're off to see the wizard, the wonderful wizard of Oz . . ."

After picking up Marcia at her junior high school, we drove downtown to the Jayhawk Theater, where *The Wizard of Oz,* in rerelease, had just opened. It was a rare treat, and the three of us giggled as the theater darkened and the movie lit up the screen.

Some weeks later our Buick sedan raced alongside a Santa Fe passenger train speeding toward Kansas City from Topeka. Tracks and highway ran along the river, and horses and cattle grazed in nearby fields. My father was driving; Marcia and I sat next to him in the front seat.

The speedometer climbed to eighty as the car pulled alongside the great engine, which flashed red and silver in the afternoon sun. The roar of the train made it hard to hear, but as usual we yelled, "Go Daddy Go! You can beat it!"

At eighty-five he slowed down, and the train disappeared around a bend. It was the Super Chief on its way from Los Angeles to Chicago. We considered it almost our own because so many members of our family worked in Santa Fe Railroad shops by the river and in offices downtown.

When we got home, Mother handed me a small pad of paper and a pencil to make a picture story about the afternoon. I filled several pages, which she stapled together. Later she placed the booklet with others in a small drawer of our living room desk.

BERKELEY — 2014

As part of my exhumation, I have unearthed from deep in the basement one of the picture books I made as a child, but I can't find the red spiral notebook I bought in the eighth grade to write a story about the Hungarian Revolution. In the fall of 1956, television images of teenagers throwing Molotov cocktails at Russian tanks caught my attention, and at the end of that year a Hungarian freedom fighter came to Topeka and spoke at our church. He was a solemn eighteen-year-old who had seen friends killed when the Soviet army attacked. Now he was traveling through the United States raising money for refugees like himself. I wanted to ask how he dared risk his life for freedom but never got the chance. In the red notebook, I wrote a long story about him, imagining what I didn't know. He told our youth group at church that he had fled to Austria across a rickety wooden bridge. I tried to picture that place. Was he alone? Did anyone meet him on the other side? How had he gotten from there to our town?

Later I saw a photograph of the Bridge at Andau, infamous for the tens of thousands of Hungarians who escaped over it before November 21, 1956, when Soviet troops blew it up.

That bridge glows in my memory, as does the freedom fighter, whose name I don't remember.

FROM THE VESTIBULE, Sally and I moved into the next car of the train. Some people were playing cards on wooden trays they had gotten from beneath their seats. A mother soothed an unhappy child. Other passengers were asleep, sitting up. It was a "chair car"—no compartments or roomettes. The train leaned into a wide turn, tossing us into the lap of a young woman in a blue sweater and skirt, dyed to match. She frowned at first, then smoothed her skirt and laughed. Sally jumped up and apologized in what seemed to me a southern accent, "Ma'am, we are very sorry."

I said nothing.

In the next chair car, we met four uniformed soldiers who said they'd boarded the train near Fort Riley, an army base west of Topeka, and were headed for Alaska.

"But we're pretty sure we'll end up in Korea," one of them said. I knew about the war in Korea from watching the news on television.

My father sometimes worried aloud about the war, but after hearing about atomic bomb drills at our schools, he told Marcia and me not to be afraid. We'd be safe, because in a nuclear conflict we'd go to our cottage up north. No one would bother to bomb Alexandria, Minnesota, he said.

As we walked forward, Sally introduced both of us to almost everyone and especially porters, who were—as far as I could tell—all African Americans. In one vestibule we encountered porter James Dodge (he wore a name tag), standing at an open window. It was snowing now, and a prairie wind blew snowflakes into the vestibule. James Dodge said he found it invigorating.

He was taller and younger than my father. I stood on tiptoe to take in the cold air and agreed it felt good. "Where do you sleep?" Sally asked. "Do you like being a porter?" He explained that he slept in "sort of a dorm in an auxiliary baggage car" next to the engine but didn't say if he liked his work. He also told us about the trip ahead. I was listening to the *clickety-clack* music of the train and heard only bits of what he said.

"I got on the Portland Rose in St. Louis. In Cheyenne, some cars, including yours, will be switched to the City of San Francisco, which is speeding north of us from Chicago right now.

"We may be delayed. A blizzard . . . Donner Pass . . . California. "

After a few minutes, Sally and I got cold in the vestibule and went forward again. Near the engine, we came to a door that looked different from the rest. The door was locked, and when we knocked, no one came. We could hear men talking and an occasional thumping.

Sally asked, "What do you think is in there?"

"Guns and snakes—and we'll need to get a key to feed them because porters and conductors will be afraid." I made up explanations for what I couldn't explain.

Brakes squealed—the train was slowing down.

"I have a promise to keep," I said, and I ran back through the train to a car with elevated seats and a glass top. I sat down in the first empty chair. Sally followed and stood in the aisle to watch.

The windows were dirty, and I couldn't wipe them clean.

On the platform, a woman in a heavy coat and feathered hat walked from the station toward the train, her face shadowed by the hat.

Please let her take it off, I thought.

She walked up and down, seeking her assigned car, and for a moment, the shadow lifted from her face. I cried out in disappointment. Then I saw people getting out of a car in a parking lot. They came toward the train and passed under my window. I studied each person's face and sank back into my seat.

Sally asked why I was crying.

I told her to leave me alone, and seconds later she did. I heard the door of the car wheeze shut behind her and thought, "Perhaps I do want her as a friend."

Leaving the station, the train rocked gently—a ship on a prairie sea. I sat for a while thinking about the promise I had made. Was it too hard to keep? When I returned to our compartment, my father was sitting in the chair looking back toward home. He asked if I'd felt the locomotive pulling harder than before.

"The Kansas prairie tilts up toward Denver," he said, "which is a mile high. The engine is straining a little as we climb." I looked over his shoulder and saw the incline. I also saw horses and cows left outside in pastures on this snowy day. We passed a farmer pitching hay to cattle from a truck. He waved, and I frowned in response.

"It's wrong, Daddy, don't you think? They should be in barns."

"They've got thick coats, Elizabeth. Don't worry. They prefer winter to summer bugs and heat."

I studied women's faces at stations in Ellis, Oakley, and Sharon Springs, recognizing the names of the towns because my father had taught me to read a Union Pacific timetable. The list of stops and estimated times of arrival appealed to me—a journey of eighteen hundred miles reduced to a single page. We were nearing a state, Colorado, where I'd never been before. Wyoming was next, then Utah, Nevada, and California.

It would be sunny in California, my father said. We'd see flowers called birds of paradise and eat lemons fresh from trees.

"We'll feel better. You'll see."

We got off the train in Denver and, because of engine trouble on our Portland Rose, spent several hours in Union

Station. I liked the café and the store full of books and news-papers. For a long time we sat on a wooden bench watching people rush to and from trains. I looked closely at each woman. My father noticed but didn't ask what I was doing. He often said I had the right to my own thoughts.

Back aboard the train, as we sped north from Denver to Cheyenne, a bright moon hung low over the Rockies. I was reading *The Road to Oz,* and Daddy interrupted to show me a high peak that glistened in the cold light. It was no longer snowing, and the world seemed frozen to a stop, except for us. In the book, Dorothy was showing a new friend named Button Bright how to wind up Tik-tok—his "thinking machine first, then his speech, and finally his action; so he would doubtless run perfectly until they had reached the Emerald City."

I wondered if people could be wound up and brought back to life.

"Good night, Louie," I said, closing the book. "Good night, Daddy.

"Good night, Mommy."

HAITI—1994

We drive slowly along a dirt road next to the Port-au-Prince International Airport.

The last flight out of Haiti took off last night, and the island is now cut off from the outside. UN-sponsored negotiations are failing; an invasion of US troops is imminent. The United Nations, the Organization of American States, and the Clinton administration are determined to restore President Jean-Bertrand Aristide to power. The military junta that overthrew him three years ago has declared a state of siege.

We need a few shots of the deserted airport for a *NewsHour* story.

Suddenly—an open gate. We drive through it and stop next to a runway. The crew and our interpreter, Louis Saint-Lot, jump out to shoot while I stay back with driver André Thelussa. We're a little nervous because potential military targets like the airport are off-limits to reporters, but in our ten days of working here, those rules have not been enforced.

We get the necessary shots and are loading the gear into the car when a man comes running at us, waving his arms.

"Sir, wait, sir!" He yells.

He's an airport security official, and he's irate. As he and Louis argue in Creole, a four-door Toyota truck wheels

through the gate. Four soldiers armed with M-1s jump out
and hold us at gunpoint. Louis tells them that his uncle is
director of the airport and will be displeased to learn we've
been treated rudely. The official calls the director on a cell
phone. A half hour later he arrives—an older gentleman in
a dark suit—and assesses the situation. He's a civilian, and
the military is in charge. He tells Louis he's sorry but he
can't help.

We're under arrest for trespassing in a restricted area.
The soldiers will escort us back to our hotel, and Louis and
André will be taken somewhere else.

This is the nightmare I've prayed would never happen.
Protecting local people who help us produce pieces for *The
NewsHour* is a requirement of my work. Sometimes danger
can't be avoided, but we didn't have to go through that gate.
We'd violated a sacred trust by unnecessarily endangering
Louis and André.

John, Jaime, and I refuse to leave without them. If the
soldiers try to take them away, we'll throw ourselves under
their truck. The threat produces a tense standoff.

Finally, Louis insists that we go.

"No one will hurt me," he says, "and I will protect
André with my life. Go back to the hotel and call my wife.
She knows what to do."

Louis's brother is a colonel in the Haitian army. His father was the first Haitian ambassador to the United Nations. The family has close connections to the military government and to the opposition, which makes Louis an especially good fixer. That's what news crews call a local interpreter who also helps in other ways, like deciding when it's safe to shoot. After studying at UCLA, Louis returned to Haiti to make T-shirts for the National Football League. A UN-imposed economic embargo has made it impossible to get the cotton he needs, and his business is going broke. That's why he's working for us.

We leave with the armed men. They take us first to the Civil Aviation Building, where Lieutenant Colonel Marc Valmé, chief of airport security, confiscates our tape cassettes. They include some of John's best work so far on this trip, and he vigorously objects.

"I'm taking them instead of *you*," Valmé snarls. He's a thug, a member of the original group that overthrew Aristide.

Of the hour and twelve minutes of exposed tape, about two minutes contained footage of the airport.

From the Civil Aviation Building, a police guard escorts us to the hotel and Louis and André to the army's Twenty-Second Company headquarters, known as Fort Dimanche.

In the next days, we're forced to give up passports and press credentials and are forbidden to work. We hire an attorney, and he and Louis's wife organize a vigorous but quiet campaign to free our colleagues. At first we keep their detention secret, because the lawyer says that publicity will make their plight worse.

A Creole phrase describes how we feel: *casque zombie,* shell of a zombie.

Along with their families, we're allowed to take Louis and André food and cigarettes. They're held in the reception area of Fort Dimanche and are not mistreated. Louis thinks they will be released any minute; André is more realistic. He's a gentle seventy-two-year-old man who walked three hours from his home every morning to drive for us. He's dignified and stoic, but clearly afraid. After four days they're moved to the National Penitentiary, an infamously pestilential place.

Word about them gets out, and many people offer to help. US ambassador William Swing adds his weight, as does a high US State Department official contacted by *The NewsHour*.

Five days after the arrests, an immigration official arrives at the hotel to deport us. We refuse to leave until Louis and André are safe in their homes, but a US consular official and the Haitian attorney convince us that our deportation is a necessary face-saving device for the junta. Once we leave, Louis and André will be freed with no charges against them. The arrest has become a distraction for Haiti's leaders.

News crews gather outside the hotel. Before leaving, I tell them on camera that we believe the rulers of Haiti are using us and our crew to intimidate the media and especially courageous Haitians who have risked their lives for three violent years to cover the news.

The immigration official had promised that a US consular official could drive us in his car to the border, but at the last minute we're ordered into the bed of a Toyota pickup by two policemen, each with a .45-caliber pistol and an Uzi aimed at us. The consular official and several reporters and camera crews follow us first to the central police station, where we're fingerprinted, and then onto a highway to the Dominican Republic, which is about sixty miles away.

Halfway there, we stop at a military checkpoint, where soldiers aggressively order us to return to Port-au-Prince. Surprisingly, our police guards refuse, and after some argument, we continue toward the Dominican Republic. In all, about five hours have passed since we left the hotel. Behind us, the soldiers force the consular official and CNN's Peter Arnett, who had stayed on our tail, to go back.

Thirty minutes later we come to a place I will never forget. On one side of a high fence is Haiti, which is barren and brown, ruined by environmental degradation. On the other side is the Dominican Republic, which is exuberantly green. We sign papers in a guard shack, open a door, and walk freely to a taxi, which takes us to a hotel in Santo Domingo. The next day we fly home. On airplane monitors we watch a CNN story about our deportation.

Five days later, Louis and André are released from the penitentiary. As promised, they are not charged with any infraction. Louis tells me on the telephone that they witnessed fellow prisoners eating human excrement to keep from starving. He insists that we shouldn't blame ourselves for what happened, that something he hadn't yet discovered was responsible for our arrest.

His kind words don't help. I regret going through that open gate. For the next four years, I am glad to help anchor *The NewsHour* in Washington, D.C., interviewing domestic and foreign leaders in the studio and also many artists about their work. Working closely with Jim Lehrer, I learn important lessons, such as keeping questions short and treating people I interview with respect, no matter how much I disagree with what they're saying. Anchoring is challenging, and I enjoy the excitement of daily television production. But by 1999, I am eager to return to foreign reporting, however dangerous the assignment. After some hesitation, producer Joanne Elgart and I go to Haiti to investigate whether the US intervention that replaced Aristide has improved people's lives and security. While there, I seek more information about the 1994 arrests. I know from reports in US newspapers that Colonel Marc Valmé, chief of security at the airport when we were arrested, has been convicted in the US District Court of Miami of conspiracy to import cocaine and distribute it in the United States. Under the military junta, Haiti had become a key transit point for Colombian cocaine and heroin, and according to the indictment, Valmé ran people and drugs through the airport in Port-au-Prince.

I see Louis Saint-Lot again and tell him I now believe we were arrested on the tarmac that day because we got too close to Valmé's drug operations. Louis agrees and says that the junta then tried—unsuccessfully—to use the arrests and deportation to intimidate the local and international press.

TOPEKA — 1950–1952

One morning when I was in second grade, Mother said she was going to the hospital for a short stay. I asked, "To have a baby?" She smiled and shook her head no.

A chill settled over the house when she left and persisted after she came home. I could tell she was hurting, though she didn't complain. When I needed something, she told me to ask my father.

When I wanted to ask a friend to spend the night, she said, "Maybe another time." I wondered if she was tired of being a mother.

Marcia was busy with school and friends, and if she knew what was happening, she didn't say. I didn't ask her because I thought I should figure it out for myself.

On her fortieth birthday, Mother heard that friends were planning a surprise party and decided to surprise *them*. She enlisted me to help. We powdered her hair, and she wore old-lady clothes borrowed from my grandmother. Delighted by what she was doing, but embarrassed to be seen with her, I hid on the floor of the car when she drove me to a friend's house on her way to the party. That night she laughed as she told us that, at first, her friends hadn't recognized her.

After several months she went back to the hospital. I sometimes had to stay alone before and after school. One day I heard footsteps on the basement stairs and fled across the street to a neighbor's house. The neighbor told Daddy I was afraid, and he hired a girl from a nearby farm to stay with me when he was gone. But she had a boyfriend in town and sneaked out with him, so I was often alone.

When Mother returned, she spent a lot of time in bed. After several days, she called me into her room.

"Sit down, darling. I don't want you to be surprised."

I sat on the nubby white bedspread and saw that her eyes were dark with concern. She took off her bed jacket and revealed purple scars where breasts had been.

"The doctors removed them to make me well again. I'm all right, dear. Come now, don't cry."

In the months that followed, she got so thin I could see bones under her skin. I heard her sometimes at night coughing and throwing up in the bathroom but didn't get out of bed to help. Instead, I lay awake, praying, "Please let her be like she was before. Don't let her stay like this forever."

That's when the bellowing started—*whoosh whoosh*—louder and louder, night after night. I cried for help as the monster came near, but no sounds came out.

One morning I got up early and went to my parents' room. Mother asked for a kiss; I refused. My father stood with his back to us, watching in the mirror above her dresser.

"Will Mother ever get well?"

"Yes," he answered.

"What does Granddad say?" My mother's father was a surgeon, gruff and unsentimental.

"Granddad is not my doctor," Mother said. "Don't worry—I'll get better soon."

ON THE SECOND morning of our trip, my father woke up late because he hadn't slept well. In Cheyenne, a steam engine had noisily switched our car and others from the Portland Rose to the City of San Francisco and kept him awake.

He said that because we were now traveling in an elegant, extra-fare streamliner, I should wear a dress and new shoes to breakfast. I resisted, but he prevailed.

"What's a streamliner?"

"A train streamlined to go fast."

"What does streamlined mean?"

"I think it means the engine and cars are designed to move smoothly through the air, like a stream."

We walked to the diner through swaying cars and joined Sally and her parents at their table. My new friend sat quietly, hands folded on her lap, waiting for breakfast.

There was plush red carpet on the floor, and drapes with stripes of blue, pink, and white framed the windows. The china on the table was decorated with an image of our train as a winged chariot flying before the wind.

My father and Sally's parents talked about the trip, mentioning Sherman Summit, the highest part of our journey, which the train had climbed while we slept. Daddy said he'd heard the engines straining to reach eight thousand feet. Outside I saw a broad basin and hills turning pink as the sun climbed the sky.

I thought again about the passage of time. Does it change depending on how fast we're going?

Before leaving home, my father had read a book about the Union Pacific Railroad, and now he explained that the route we were traveling was almost one hundred years old. That's when the first transcontinental railroad got built, he said.

Just about that long ago, my Grampie's father—my great-grandfather—had moved his family by railroad from Ohio to the Dakotas, where they homesteaded. A couple of years later, a fierce blizzard wiped out their cattle, horses, and crops. The family couldn't afford to replace what they'd lost and fled south to Topeka to work for the Atchison, Topeka and Santa Fe Railway.

Grampie was five years old when the blizzard hit. He said that an ice storm blew in suddenly with a terrible fury, temporarily blinding his mother, who was pregnant, as she walked from the barn to their sod house. Somehow she found the clothesline and followed it to the door. The extreme cold of the blizzard froze cattle and horses where they stood and killed children on their way to school. It's called the Children's Blizzard in some history books. When the snow melted, brothers and sisters were found frozen to death, locked in each other's arms.

My great-grandfather farmed and also taught. He and his students, stranded for three days in their schoolhouse, survived. My great-aunt Mabel was delivered by a mid-wife during the blizzard. When Grampie told this part of the story, my cousins and I would giggle, thinking of Aunt Mabel, who now lived in Maine. A big, matronly woman, she nearly suffocated us when she hugged us against her bosom during her annual visits to Topeka.

As my father chatted with her parents, Sally leaned over and whispered, "Did the mystery car get switched to this train?" We asked to be excused and went to find out.

The City of San Francisco had thicker carpets and more colorful curtains than the Portland Rose. In the club car, we saw a bar and round tables for snacking and playing games. Another car had a barbershop and a shower that any passenger could use. In one of the chair cars we saw the woman whose lap we'd fallen into the day before. I liked her pink sweater set and gray wool skirt. She said she was a nurse in St. Louis and was traveling to San Francisco to see if she liked it. If she did, she'd move sometime later in the year.

As before, we found the mystery car near the front of the train. Again, when we knocked, no one answered. We heard low voices and the same pounding and thumping as before. After waiting a few minutes, we went back to find James Dodge, figuring he'd have a key, but he refused to help.

"You shouldn't go where you don't belong."

I heard the squeal of brakes and felt the train slowing down. I had a promise to keep. It was time to search again.

CHILE — SEPTEMBER 1970

Am I here because of what I witnessed in Peru six years ago?

The summer after my junior year at Middlebury, I worked with an American nurse in the only clinic of a shantytown on the edge of Trujillo, Peru. Five thousand people lived in that *barriada,* with little access to health care, sewage systems, schools, adequate water, or enough food. The Peruvian friend I was visiting served as a translator three afternoons a week in the clinic, and I took temperatures and did other small jobs. In my first week, a doctor came to help the nurse inoculate two hundred people against diphtheria. I noticed that many babies had infected scabs on their bodies. "No soap and little water for washing," the nurse explained.

One day as we were leaving, a woman came running down the road and blocked our van. "Come quickly," she said. "My sister is dying."

We followed and found a young mother of three bleeding from a self-inflicted abortion. Her children didn't have enough to eat, she said. How could she feed another? We got her to a hospital; she survived.

I decided then that I had an obligation as a human being to try to help ease such suffering, and now I'm in Santiago helping produce a film about a presidential election that features a candidate who promises to do that. My husband, an attorney, is back in California, traveling from strike to strike on behalf of Cesar Chavez's United Farm Workers. Jenny, our twenty-two-month-old daughter, has come to Chile with me.

It's the last night of campaigning, and hundreds of thousands of people wait to hear Salvador Allende speak from an immense wooden stage in downtown Santiago. He has run unsuccessfully for president three times before, almost winning once. Polls indicate that this time he may defeat candidates from both the Conservative and Christian Democratic Parties.

Allende's coalition, Unidad Popular—Popular Unity—includes his own Socialist Party, the centrist Radical Party, and the Communist Party, among others. I see luminaries from those parties on the stage. Pablo Neruda sits down next to Allende as introductions begin.

We have three crews covering the event. I'm standing just below the stage with Gustavo Moris, the lead cameraman. He frowns as people behind us test the rope barricade that separates us and other media from the crowd. When Allende is introduced, a mass of people surges forward and the rope breaks. Gustavo uses his girth to protect me from being crushed and hoists me and the camera onto the stage before clambering up himself. Director Saul Landau and producer Jim Becket are already there. As the stage begins to sway, Saul says, "The whole f—ing thing is going to collapse."

Pushed to the edge, I jump off, but Saul, Jim, and Gustavo stay on the unstable structure. Gustavo keeps filming. Allende, who had taken the microphone to calm the crowd, begins to speak. The stage holds. I make my way to the front again to help cameraman Jorge Müller get shots of our people mixing with the crowd. We're making a fictional film that will also include documentary footage—like *Medium Cool,* a Hollywood film directed by Saul's friend Haskell Wexler. On cue, the actors playing a Peace Corps volunteer and her revolutionary Chilean lover come face to face with a tall American man they think may be a CIA agent. Jorge gets a shot of the three of them warily shaking hands.

In his speech, Allende promises land reform and the nationalization of American copper companies in Chile. He's authoritative but warm—like a grandfather. As a physician, he has special credibility when he describes chronic malnutrition and promises free milk for children. He calls for good relations with Cuba, which would break its hemispheric isolation. This part of his platform especially infuriates the Nixon administration.

When Allende finishes, the cheers from the crowd are deafening. People around us jump up and down and shout, "El que no salta es momio. El que no salta es momio" (He who doesn't jump is a mummy [reactionary])—a demonstration of joyful support.

Jorge and I walk through the crowd filming heated discussions of the speech.

I've never been among such passionate, politically engaged people. They all seem to have read Marx, Lenin, and Che Guevara. Allende is a Marxist democrat, which some consider a contradiction in terms. He calls for a "Chilean way to socialism," a peaceful exit from imperialist exploitation. A campaign poster reads, "They took the copper and left us the holes," referring to the American copper companies that control much of Chile's most important natural resource.

I ask Jorge what he thinks about the speech and the crowd's reaction. He's twenty-three, with long curly hair and the facial features of a classical Greek statue. His German father fled the Holocaust; his mother is Chilean. He comes at night with a guitar to jam with other musicians at the house where we Americans in the crew are staying. Now he lowers the camera, looks around, and says, "If Allende wins, the Right won't give up without a struggle. What will happen to these people then?"

Later, driving back to our house, I see long lines of Allende supporters walking quietly in the dark. I know that some live in shantytowns many miles away. They'll get little sleep before work in the morning.

Two days later, Salvador Allende wins a plurality but not a majority of the vote. The right-wing candidate, Jorge Alessandri, is runner-up, and by law the Chilean congress must choose between the two men. In the past, the congress has chosen the candidate with the most votes.

Now, several weeks later, I'm in the kitchen with Jenny and the maids in the mansion where we live. It's a poorly preserved white stucco Spanish-style house with eight bedrooms and a swimming pool full of leaves and dirty water. To get dollars in case they decide to flee Chile, the wealthy owners have moved out of their home and rented it to us for three months, along with two maids and a nanny.

Jenny is speaking full sentences now—Spanish and English. She likes the nanny but is sometimes overwhelmed by the fifteen Americans who live in our house and by the Chilean crew who make it their headquarters as well. I'm in charge of running the household, among other jobs, so I get to be with her a lot, but I know she misses our life as a small family in California.

The doorbell rings, and Jenny comes with me to open the door. Luciano Cruz is there, flanked by an even larger man, perhaps a bodyguard. Cruz is as handsome in person as in photographs. He's a leader of a 1960s-style group known as the Movement of the Revolutionary Left (MIR). Some of the Chileans in our crew support MIR, but most do not. It has carried out acts of violence that could harm the prospects of the electoral Left, the critics of MIR say. Luciano Cruz asks politely if he can talk to the directors about our movie. He doesn't like what he's heard about the script. Saul and Jim come from upstairs, and I watch as Cruz places his .45-caliber semiautomatic pistol on the couch and then sits down. Before Jenny and I return to the kitchen, I hear him say that he believes an Allende victory will eventually have to be defended with arms.

Chile has a long tradition of peaceful transitions of power, and I hope Cruz will be proven wrong.

But the morning after Allende won the plurality, when I went to the Bank of America to get cash for house and production expenses, I found the door locked, with no indication when the bank might reopen. Also, the grocery store had run out of some staples. While I was shopping, the lights went out for several minutes, and people cried out in fear. Chile's influential daily *El Mercurio* says that flights to America and Europe are sold out. Wealthy Chileans are fleeing "a communist takeover."

We have heard rumors that the CIA is paying for scare pieces in newspapers to create economic chaos and insecurity. Some say the Chilean right wing, with help from the United States, will foment a military coup to prevent Congress from confirming Allende as president.

As BRAKES GRABBED hold and the train slowed down, I told Sally we should study the mystery car from outside. We got coats from our compartments and went to the vestibule at the end of a car where James Dodge was opening the door.

"No getting off unless you're with a parent," he said. We waited until he was busy with other people and then jumped from the steps to the platform.

The mystery car looked different than others on the train. It seemed longer and had a wide sliding door on the side, flanked by two small windows, each covered by a shade.

"Is it a cattle car?" Sally asked.

In Topeka, I sometimes walked down to look at the cattle cars on railroad tracks near my grandparents' house. Through open slats, I could see cows crowded together with no water and little room to move. This was no cattle car.

"Let's find a rock and throw it at the window," I suggested. "Maybe someone will come."

"No." Sally frowned. "The window might break." Instead, I tossed up gravel from under the train and got the reaction we wanted. A shade flew up, and a young man in a cowboy hat appeared. He looked about eighteen, a little older than my sister. I waved, and he nodded and started to smile, but then a shadow moved behind him and a hand yanked down the shade.

"Whoever did that is hiding something," I told Sally.

We waited for a few minutes, but the shade stayed down. Sally returned to the warmth of the train, and I walked forward, past mail and baggage cars, stopping for a few minutes by the locomotive, which shook and growled like a huge animal. The engineer waved and shouted something I couldn't understand. A sign on the redbrick station read, "Rawlins, Wyoming." I went to the doorway and stood for a moment, looking around. A man asked if I needed help, and then movement across the street caught my eye. In the window of a small house, I saw a woman brushing her hair and pinning it up. She looked like my mother.

I ran toward her across the street and sprinted up a path to the house as the conductor called, "All aboard!" The engineer blew the horn and then blew it again. The woman opened the front door, and we stared at each other.

"I thought you might be someone else," I said, and turned back toward the train. The conductor was waving frantically for me to come. I ran as fast I could, and when I got to him, he reached down and pulled me into the vestibule as wheels began to turn.

My father came down the aisle, scowling. He had seen what happened. In our compartment, he spoke sternly. "What were you looking for? It's selfish to make everyone wait."

I couldn't tell him the truth, so I said nothing. He confined me for two hours to the room, and I read to my bear, Louie, again:

Tik-tok was popular with the people of Oz because he was so trustworthy, reliable and true; he was sure to do exactly what he was wound up to do, at all times, and in all circumstances. Perhaps it is better to be a machine that does its duty than a flesh-and-blood person who will not, for a dead truth is better than a live falsehood.

When the two hours ended, I went to Sally's room for a game of hide-and-seek with Louie and our Toni dolls. She'd also been given a Toni doll for Christmas.

"My doll is nine years old, and yours is her mother," I dictated. "The mother disappears and my doll must find her."

"Why did the mother disappear?"

I thought for a minute. "I don't know, but Louie, the detective, will find out."

I covered my eyes while Sally hid her doll. Louie found it quickly in Sally's overnight bag. The room was too small for this game, so we spent the rest of the afternoon looking out the window. From the sparkling air, we knew that it was

very cold. We passed over a rushing river and saw spires of rock that changed color as we approached. I lost track of time, and late in the afternoon we pulled into a small station with a sign that said, "Green River, Wyoming, population 4,020."

Two women came out of the station, and I stood up in Sally's compartment to better see their faces. They came close to the window, looking for their car.

"It's not her," I whispered before sitting back down.

SAUDI ARABIA — JANUARY 2002

Fever hallucinations in the Abha Palace Hotel.

I wake up sick, and my temperature is rising. Producer Joanne Elgart is running the show. Two days ago, angry men chased her and the crew from the mosque where some of the nineteen hijackers from the 9/11 attack had worshipped. The provincial governor, a member of the royal family, demanded that we accept an armed guard. We resisted, but yesterday a large man appeared in the hotel lobby to accompany us when we leave the hotel. He carries an M-16 and a pistol and has two knives stuck in an ammunition belt across his chest.

The NewsHour has been on emergency footing since 9/11. My twenty-six-year-old son, Sam, who had just arrived in New York for graduate school, was staying in Battery Park about a block from the World Trade Center. Pieces of the first airplane crashed through the window of an apartment in his building. When the towers fell, he fled through choking debris, running south until a ferry picked him up and took him across the East River to Brooklyn.

At first I did live interviews almost every day from the San Francisco *NewsHour* studio, focusing on Al Qaeda and Afghanistan. In November, I reported from Cairo, home of Mohamed Atta, who piloted American Airlines Flight 11 into the North Tower. With producer Mary Jo Brooks, I interviewed leaders of the Muslim Brotherhood and human rights activists, among others. Soldiers detained and questioned us for several hours near a military prison outside Cairo, and a small group of Islamist men made it clear with hostile comments that we weren't welcome in their neighborhood. Otherwise the shoot went smoothly.

Two months later, I reported on the second Intifada in Israel and the West Bank. One day, while we filmed outside Arafat's headquarters in Ramallah, an Israeli tank spun its turret and aimed a large gun at us. The following afternoon, in the same place, producer Morgan Till, the camera crew, and the fixer got caught between stone-throwing Palestinian demonstrators and Israeli soldiers, who fired rubber-coated bullets at first and later live ammunition. Our group returned unharmed to the hotel, where an editor and I were finishing a piece for the program that night. We added the new footage. More than thirty people were wounded that day, some seriously.

After feeding the story via satellite to *The NewsHour,* I couldn't sleep. I am more worried now than I've ever been about the safety of people I work with. In my past experience, journalists rarely became direct targets, no matter how violent the conflict. Now, in some places, we're seen as the enemy. A cameraman is especially at risk because a large video camera resembles a gun.

A week ago, the crew and I drove from Jerusalem across the Allenby Bridge to Amman, Jordan, and then flew to Riyadh, Saudi Arabia. Producer Joanne Elgart had arrived earlier. She and I are required to cover ourselves with abaya and hijab, and in some hotels we must eat separately from the crew in a women's dining room. We may not—by law— drive a car. I feel uncomfortable and constrained much of the time.

In Jeddah we produced a profile of architect Sami Angawi, a descendant of the Prophet Mohammed. Angawi had designed a large family home that reflects the dualities he believes Islam embraces. The house feels private, yet open to the world, like a Catholic cathedral. Most doors and windows are screened, but light permeates every room, flowing through lattices that evoke both Islam and Christianity.

"As you walk from one part to another, it's like walking in my mind," Angawi said. "I see things in layers, in details. I look at our Islamic culture from different perspectives."

He believes Islamic civilization was great in the past because it was open to many influences and traditions. He's worried that in today's Saudi Arabia, Islam has become too restricted.

"The way it's taught is mainly in one direction, one view."

According to a survey carried out by Saudi Intelligence, 95 percent of educated Saudis ages twenty-five to forty-one support what Osama Bin Laden did on 9/11.

"My son and his friends were in the house three days after the incident," Angawi said. "I asked what they think of Bin Laden. They shrugged their shoulders. A week later, they were also here, and one of them said, 'You asked about Bin Laden, and we didn't tell you. You know what? We think he's a hero.'"

Nine of the fifteen Saudis among the nineteen hijackers came from southwestern Saudi Arabia, where we are now. Of those, five came from this provincial capital, Abha, or nearby villages.

In bed sick now, in the hotel, I think of Sam's description of body parts beneath his New York window, how a waiter from a nearby restaurant ran to cover remains with white napkins and tablecloths.

We are among the first American journalists to get into the kingdom since the attacks. When we say we'd like to contact families of the hijackers, our fixer says it's not possible.

I hope my fever breaks soon.

OVER CANDLELIGHT AT dinner west of Green River, Sally's mother asked me about home.

Words tumbled out: "We have a white house with green shutters, three bedrooms, and a playhouse in back under a willow tree whose branches droop almost to the ground. After school I roller-skate with friends and play games like kick-the-can. My sister Marcia could have come with us on the trip, but she had too much school-work and also didn't want to leave her horse, whose name is Flag. I've just written a letter asking her to go out to the farm where Flag and Penny live and please to put them in the barn so they don't freeze. Flag is a big red horse, and Penny, a roan, is my cousin's. I ride her now, and when I'm big, I'll get to ride Flag, who is very spirited. Cindy, our dog, comes with us to the farm and chases the pigs. There are a lot of pigs."

Daddy described his work as a Buick salesman. "The job will end soon," he said. "I was supposed to get the dealer-ship, but at the last minute, General Motors chose someone else, and I'm terribly disappointed."

He and Sally's father discovered that they were both thirty-two when the United States entered World War II. They joined as commissioned officers before being called up. Sally's dad had spent the war in something called Army Intelligence in Washington, D.C. My father taught gunnery at naval air stations in Minneapolis, Jacksonville, and Key West. I was born in Minneapolis.

"I expected to be assigned to a ship when I chose the navy, but they discovered I get sea sick," Daddy said, laugh-ing at himself. "I'd always hunted, so they made me a gun-nery officer. I taught boys how to lead when they shoot, preparing them for air combat. I wish I knew which ones survived."

As he and Sally's father talked, the young man from the mystery car came down the corridor. He was tall and skinny, with narrow shoulders and hips, and he wore cowboy boots, a dark blue shirt, and jeans. As he passed, he attracted attention. Heads turned. He stopped next to me.

"I saw you staring at our car at the station in Rawlins. What did you want?"

One of his eyes twitched. *Was he nervous?* Sally kicked me under the table—*whap whap*—a warning not to reveal our interest in whatever he was hiding, because our parents wouldn't want us snooping. I looked at my father and shrugged as if to say, "I don't know what he's talking about."

"They don't mean any harm," my father said. "They're curious about *every*thing."

The cowboy stared at me, and when I still didn't speak, he nodded, as though he'd learned something from my silence.

The train has become wondrous. He's uncanny, a boy-man wise beyond his years.

As he moved to a table across the aisle, a shorter man in a shiny gray suit came down the corridor. He was about my father's age and wore red shoes. I had never seen red shoes on a man before. He sat down next to the cowboy. They were clearly traveling together.

"That must be who pulled down the shade," I whispered to Sally. "Something strange is happening. Let's sneak a note to our guy."

After dinner, we asked to be excused and got a piece of paper from the head steward. I wrote, "We think you need help. Meet us in one hour in the observation car." The steward offered to pass the note to the cowboy "surreptitiously."

"What's that mean?"

"Secretly."

In the observation car, with its glass roof, the moon bathed us in light as it moved west with the train.

"I don't think he'll come," Sally said as we waited.

The hour passed and then two more minutes, then ten. The train raced forward—*clickety-clack, clickety-clack, clickety-clack*. Finally the door opened, and we heard footsteps on the stairs. The tall cowboy stood looking down at us, and then he asked, "What makes you think I need help?"

"You're traveling in a locked car, which means you're hiding something," I answered. "We think you've been kidnapped by that other man."

He laughed out loud, stepped over Sally, and sat down between us.

"Imagine that! You've been spying! I thought so. And you're not all wrong. I haven't been kidnapped, and I don't need your help, but we do have a secret. You should stay away from our car."

A secret!

I wanted to ask more but sensed he'd revealed all he could. We sat in silence for a few minutes until he unfolded himself and—without saying good-bye—disappeared down the aisle.

The moon had moved on, leaving us in darkness. Sally and I were alone in the observation car. No one came to turn on lights.

She asked, "What could the secret be? Snakes like you thought before?"

"I don't know, but we've got to find out."

CHILE — OCTOBER 1970

Cast and crew have gone north for a week to film in Copiapó. I'll join them in a couple of days to portray a Peace Corps volunteer working with children in a shantytown. The other character in the scene is played by the lead actress of the film. In the movie, the CIA agent has used her to get access to a popular radical priest, who will soon be assassinated. Singer Country Joe McDonald is also in Copiapó, portraying himself. His songs in the film critique the emotional manipulation of scenes like the killing of the priest. Joe is a one-man Brechtian chorus. Directors Saul Landau and Nina Serrano are fans of Bertolt Brecht.

I like and admire Joe. From the time he arrived, he made friends with Chileans and worked hard to understand their varying points of view. I admire the film's producers and directors (who also wrote the script) for their foresight in featuring a villain from the CIA. But I do not like some of the dialogue or characterizations and fear the movie will make us seem superficial and frivolous. Also, making Brechtian points when so much is at stake seems wrong.

The American directors hope the CIA spy angle will attract a large audience in the United States, but that seems unlikely, because Raúl Ruiz, the Chilean codirector, is making a very different film, a nuanced study of several men of the Left who obsessively debate questions of revolutionary strategy. Raúl's scenes will be intercut with the American spy story, and perhaps the mix will work, but I'm pessimistic.

Jenny and I are sitting at the kitchen table, listening to the radio with Carmencha, the cook. She's a longtime member of the Communist Party and a strong supporter of the Allende coalition. Last week we shot a scene in her house in a slum on the edge of Santiago and saw why she's grateful to work for us. A single mother of three children, she needs money, and we pay and treat her better than her former bosses.

Suddenly, she cries out, "They've shot General Schneider!"

I turn up the volume. A reporter is excitedly describing a failed attempt to kidnap General René Schneider, commander in chief of the army, who resisted his assailants and got shot three times at close range. Carmencha moans as if she were wounded.

I find a member of the Chilean crew still in town, and in the next days we film outside the military hospital where the general was taken. Media from around the world and hundreds of Chileans join the deathwatch. Schneider's assailants were apparently trying to get him out of the way because, as a constitutionalist, he was blocking a military coup.

On October 24, the Chilean congress overwhelmingly confirms Allende as president, and the day after that, General Schneider dies. The cameraman and I are at the military hospital when Allende comes to pay his respects. He projects confidence, but with Schneider's death, the new president has lost one of the few military leaders he can trust.

TOPEKA—1953

On a cold, foggy morning, I pedaled my bicycle home after spending the night with cousins and found my father upstairs in his bedroom, weeping. He stood by Mother's empty bed, dialing the phone, and put the receiver down when I walked in.

"I was calling Aunt Mabel in Maine," he said. "We lost Mother last night. Nothing could be done. She's gone."

Tears streamed down his face.

Lost? Gone?

Two days before she had asked me to read from *The Road to Oz* as she lay very ill in bed. The book was still on her table.

Down the hall, Marcia was crying. Nothing made sense. My father put his arms around me, and then I fled into my room, grabbed Louie, and held him tightly to my chest.

"It can't be true," I told the bear. "She's gone some-where for reasons we don't understand. We must search for her. We'll find her—I promise."

A few days later, at the funeral, I counted the small pieces of stained glass in the church's Tiffany windows. When I reached seventy-five, I stopped for a moment and looked around. Every pew, including in the balcony, was full. Daddy said that more than three hundred people had come. Bits of red, like rubies, danced over the congregation.

There was a rectangular box at the front of the church. If she were inside, they'd have let me say good-bye, I thought. My grandmother pulled me close. She and most of the family were crying.

I kept counting and soon got up to 315.

Not long after that, the weather warmed up a little, and my father asked my sister and me to go with him to the farm to check on Penny and Flag. I knew it was an excuse to get us out of the house and lift our spirits. Marcia had gotten her license, and she drove the Buick with Daddy next to her in front. I sat in back with our dog, Cindy.

"There's the college," I told Cindy as we drove down Twenty-First Street to Burlingame Avenue. "And there's the pond where we ice-skate."

The horses were in the pasture where Shunganunga Creek ran through the property. Marcia had brought sugar cubes to catch them, and we led them back to the barn to be saddled and bridled. I helped tighten the girth of Penny's saddle and got on her back. With Daddy and Cindy walking alongside, Marcia and I started down a well-worn path that wound through several farms along the stream.

After about an hour, a whistle blew, sharp and distinct in the winter air, and the earth rumbled. Daddy said it was the Santa Fe El Capitan, coming from Los Angeles via Albuquerque. I gave Penny a gentle kick, assuming we would race the train.

Incapacitated by grief—and perhaps by fear for us—my father called, "Stop!"

The great machine roared by, shaking the ground. We walked the horses back to the barn, unsaddled them, and drove home.

VIETNAM — 1990

As dusk descends, the hum of crickets soothes the night. Warm air surrounds us like a womb. I'm walking a muddy path in central Vietnam with cameraman John Knoop, soundman Jaime Kibben, an interpreter-fixer from Hanoi, and a self-appointed village guide. Fireflies dart above us and the paddies on either side.

This is our last night in the village of Binh Phu, a string of tiny hamlets with no electricity, plumbing, or roads, and only a rudimentary school. The few books in the school were brought here from Berkeley by Thanh Pham, the subject of the film we're producing for public television. I met Thanh last year, when he served as interpreter on a story I reported for KQED in San Francisco. An American grenade had wounded him in the *American* War, as it's called here, and killed his mother and grandmother.

In an interview earlier this week, a former Viet Cong general told us that the VC had used Binh Phu as a "stepping stone" to attack Da Nang, which is about an hour away by car. "The Americans were very sensitive about the village because they knew we had stationed some of our main forces there," he said.

Thanh is staying at his aunt's house deep in the village during the shoot, but our government-appointed interpreter makes the crew and me spend nights in Da Nang because of fears for our safety. At first I feared this would doom the film. We would have to drive south for an hour and then walk almost two more hours each day to meet Thanh where he was staying. How would we get the video we needed if we were moving so much of the time?

I was wrong to worry. The path through Binh Phu is a magic lantern of images for our story.

We began the shoot five days ago at a meeting with village leaders in a concrete town hall about half a mile from the highway that runs north and south the length of Vietnam. Thanh was nervous as we all sat down. He wasn't sure how we'd be received.

Like him, the officials were in their mid-thirties. They received us dressed in farmers' clothes, tired after a night of events kicking off the Tet holiday. At first they were reticent and suspicious. Had any of us fought in Vietnam during the war?

No, we said, but close friends and relatives had.

Tran Quoc Hung, the commune president, probed further. We knew he had grown up in a family of Viet Minh fighters and joined the Viet Cong at age fifteen. He asked Thanh's American "father" why he had taken Thanh in. "Did someone make you do it?"

Father Jones, a sixty-four-year-old Episcopal priest from Berkeley with a keen sense of humor, smiled and said no. His family had responded to a request from the Committee of Responsibility, the American aid group that rescued Thanh after he was wounded and got him airlifted to San Francisco. There, an operation saved his life.

"We knew he would need special care, and we wanted to help," Father Jones said. "Besides, he was very cute."

The officials laughed. "You have the heart of a humanist," the commune president said, welcoming us warmly to Binh Phu.

Later we understood why the commune president was suspicious. His father and three uncles had been killed fighting in the war. In 1965 Americans had bombed and destroyed his school. He could still name the twenty-two students in his last classroom. Only three had survived the war. Some had died fighting for the Viet Cong; others for the South Vietnamese army. But most were noncombatants, he said.

Hung said he'd witnessed Thanh's father's death. American bombing had made it impossible to farm, and villagers were starving. They organized a march to the nearest firebase as a protest. American and South Vietnamese troops intercepted the protesters and began firing. "A friend of Thanh's father was killed," Hung said, "and Thanh's father picked up his body and continued to walk forward. Then a soldier hit him from behind with a big stick. He fell down and died."

After the meeting, we hiked deeper into the village. First one, then five, then twenty children came running from huts and paddies to join us. They giggled at our eyes and attempts to speak Vietnamese.

We're the first Americans in the village since the war ended.

An elderly woman approached with the children, yelling and shaking her fist.

"She's swearing at you," the interpreter said. She's saying, "Your people did this to me. See what your people did to me!"

She grabbed my hand and ran my fingers over bumps where fingers had been.

"I was working in a paddy when the village was bombed by an American plane. My mother died with her stomach split open, and my son's head was cut off by the bomb. My other son was wounded, and now he is too weak to work. We don't have enough to eat. Do you want to see the hole the bomb made? Come, I will take you."

The crater was a round depression in the earth about six feet in diameter. It felt alien and sinister, and I wouldn't have mistaken it for a pond, which it resembled. Banana

trees and elephant grass masked most of the damage from the bomb. Just beyond the crater, on the other side of the trail, we filmed a bridge across a drainage ditch built from pieces of wood and a rusting M-60 machine gun. Our village guide said that shortly before we arrived, a farmer in the village had died when his hoe exploded an M-79 grenade.

As we walked, more children came running. They skipped and played beside us as Thanh told stories. He remembered when the first American troops arrived.

"They came in 1963 or 1964 to help the South Vietnamese army build a camp to relocate the villagers. The Viet Cong liberated the camp and then controlled this whole area. They were basically local people, and most of the village supported them."

I saw small mounds along the path and asked Thanh what they were.

"Graves dug under fire when the village was attacked."

Near those mounds, among trees and undergrowth, were more bomb craters—so many I eventually lost count.

ASLEEP IN MY upper berth after talking to the cowboy, I dreamed that I stood before a silken veil through which I saw a shimmering, viscous world. While I watched, one perfect animal after another (horse, tiger, elephant) came out of that world toward me and then disappeared into the darkness. I tried but failed to pass into the shining place they came from and cried out.

My father stood by the side of my berth and took me in his arms.

"Elizabeth, you're dreaming. Wake up. I'm here."

"I want Mommy. I want her right now."

"You've been looking for her, haven't you?"

When I didn't respond, he said. "I am sorry—so very sorry—we didn't tell you more." He was also crying. "She's *dead*, gone from us forever. We can't bring her back. Granddad recommended we not tell you she was dying. He thought it would be worse for you to know."

It was the first time anyone had used the word *dead* when talking about my mother. At the church, the minister said she "passed on." Everyone used the word *gone*. Now the terrible word, *dead*, hovered between me and my father. I could almost see it in the room.

"It can't be true," I insisted. "How could she ask me to read to her one night and be *dead* two days later?"

"Her illness got worse, and she was unconscious at the end. We thought it best to leave you at your cousin's house during those last days. I should have explained more from the beginning. I'm sorry—very very sorry."

With my father by my side, I buried my head in the pillow and wept as the City of San Francisco raced under a black sky through the desert from Utah into Nevada.

SPAIN — 2006

In Madrid, on a shoot for *The Judge and the General* with an unusually loose schedule, Magnus Macedo, Brian Kelly, and I spend a lot of time drinking and talking in bars. Magnus is a soundman/editor and Brian is a cameraman. We've reported from difficult places together and are close friends. Two months ago, in Iraq, Magnus narrowly escaped injury from the IED that seriously wounded ABC anchorman Bob Woodruff and also injured cameraman Doug Vogt. Magnus helped save their lives and still suffers from that experience and others almost as bad. His magnetism has gotten us out of a lot of scrapes, but now he is flat, depressed, without energy. Brian, also usually a charmer, says he is flashing back to images of dead children in Sabra and Shatila, among other places he's covered. Both men have sought help for PTSD and say they're getting better. I have been spared open warfare, but as we talk through the night, I realize that death is now the common denominator of our friendship.

I WOKE UP early the morning after my father talked to me about my mother's death. The train wasn't moving, and he said we'd been stopped for some time. A curtain of snow made it impossible to see where we were. I remembered the conversation of the night before, as did he.

"I know we both feel awful," he said, "but we've got to keep going. Let's get breakfast and find out why we're not moving."

In the dining car, the head steward explained that we'd pulled off on a siding east of Reno to wait until tracks across the mountains of California could be cleared of ice and snow. "Donner Pass seldom closes for very long," he said, "but this blizzard is dumping record amounts of snow, and winds are blowing with hurricane force."

"That's eighty or ninety miles per hour," Daddy told me. "Like a tornado at home."

Sally asked what I thought would happen if we stopped for a long time.

"They'll need help in the mystery car," I answered.

Five hours later, our fifteen-car train, pulled by three diesel engines, slowly climbed Donner Pass and stopped at Norden, which Daddy said was seven thousand feet high. Through the blowing snow, I saw the dim outline of small buildings.

James Dodge came to the doorway. "Top officials of the Southern Pacific have come from San Francisco because of the emergency, and some of them are working over there," he said, pointing to one of the buildings. "In spite of almost constant plowing, we've got about five feet of drifted snow on the track right now. An eastbound train got stuck this morning, but eventually it got through. This is the worst storm I've seen, but we'll make it to Oakland. We always do."

As we started moving again, Daddy talked about the construction of this part of the railroad, and I knew he was trying to distract me from the storm. He explained how workers from China had dynamited through mountains to make room for railroad tracks.

I held Louie close as the train passed through several snow sheds many miles long and then, after a few minutes, entered a tunnel that seemed to go on forever. The roar of the engines reverberated off the walls of the tight space and reminded me of the bellowing that awakened me in the night at home. I closed my eyes and clutched my bear. Had the monster, the monkey with the motor on its tail, followed us from home?

Just beyond the tunnel, the noise faded. The train moved more slowly.

Wham!

We hit something and stopped. Louie and I pitched forward, but Daddy kept us from falling. "A drift," he said, "like running into a wall." The engines revved, and the train lurched forward. *Wham!* Another wall.

Outside—bent and broken trees and snow blowing wildly.

A sound then—like a shot—and the earth shook. Something above us broke loose, and an avalanche of ice and snow slammed into the train. We slid sideways on the seat as the car tipped and then righted again. Lights went out, and our bedroom darkened. The train was quiet. Lights came back on. Engines roared and traction motors struggled to take hold. We heard a terrible grinding. The train lurched back and forth.

"The engineer is trying to break us free," my father said.

Couplings—the joints between cars—rammed together. I thought of horses in pain.

My father tightened his grip on me. I clutched Louie. I couldn't see out our window. Were we buried in snow?

Will we die here? Will I find Mother in heaven?

VIETNAM — 1990

We've come almost to the end of the path through Binh Phu. The sky is black; villagers have blown out candles and lanterns in their homes. Frogs still croak in the paddies. The guide is singing a song of love and war, and I feel like I'm floating on his music through the humid air. I think of the overgrown trail far behind us, where Thanh led us to his mother's and grandmother's graves, barely visible in a field of deep grasses surrounded by trees. Before the war, ten

families lived in that place, but now it was eerily quiet and deserted. Villagers shun it for fear of unexploded mines and ammunition. After cleaning the graves, Thanh lit incense and wept. Later, as we sat together under a mango tree, he pointed to nearby hills.

"The Americans were stationed along those ridges. They would fire on us just for being in the paddies.

"A large battle began at dawn after Tet in 1968. I was twelve years old. They came in with helicopters and tanks, and my mother, grandmother, sister, a neighbor, and I ran into the neighbor's bomb shelter. The shooting went on for many hours. The common practice was to come out and show ourselves as soon as one side approached the shelter door. When the firing subsided and we heard the tracks of tanks, we started out. Just as I approached the door with the three women in front of me by a couple of feet, I saw lightning and explosions, and the next second it was all dark. I couldn't see anything. All I could smell was powder, and I realized the three women were dead. My shirt was wet with blood. I was wounded. I didn't know what happened to my sister.

"I came out when firing stopped because I was thirsty. Three guys came down the trail—two Americans with a Vietnamese alongside. I rushed toward them and they knocked me down and had two gun barrels on my back. They started asking questions. I tried to talk, but nothing came out."

The grenade had severed Thanh's esophagus. An American medic bandaged his throat and had him airlifted by helicopter to a Da Nang hospital, where, weeks later, a volunteer from the Committee of Responsibility found him near death from starvation and got him on a transport plane to San Francisco full of wounded soldiers.

In Oakland, before leaving for Vietnam, we filmed Thanh studying a US Army map of Vietnam with Hal Bell, who had commanded a company stationed at a firebase on a ridge near Binh Phu.

Bell asked Thanh if any "enemy soldiers" had entered the village in the days before the attack.

Thanh: "Oh yeah. The VC came in a few days before."

Bell: "That's why you got hit. Sorry."

Thanh: "Well—living in the wrong place at the wrong time, I guess. But that was our home."

After a pause, an anguished Bell said, "Jesus! I know. There were no front lines in Vietnam. I can imagine a situation where a GI, after two or three weeks of exhaustion, frustration, seeing friends killed, being harassed, never being able to close with his opponent, sees a fleeting movement out of the corner of his eye, doesn't think twice, pulls a pin and throws it. I've done it myself."

In the dark, as we walk, our guide continues to sing. The lined faces of Thanh's four aunts, the sisters of his mother, come vividly to my mind. After losing many members of their extended family, they fled to a refugee camp in a nearby town and didn't return home until after the war ended. They have faced constant hardship since then, including shortages of food when rice and potato harvests failed.

When they met Thanh's American "father," the aunts took him by the hand and welcomed him to Vietnam. "Raising Thanh after he was wounded gave him life," an aunt said. "We are grateful to you, older brother." They thought Thanh had died after the American soldiers took him away. I admire the resilience of these women who can still enjoy life in spite of losing so much.

In San Francisco, Thanh became a beloved member of the Jones family. His esophagus healed, but his throat is forever scarred and his voice hoarse. When he could eat normally again, he gained weight, learned English, played Little League baseball, and got along well in school.

But from the moment the helicopter lifted him out of Binh Phu, Thanh vowed to return home to search for surviving members of his family. By 1980, overcoming great

odds, he had saved enough money. Because he'd never left home before he was taken out in a helicopter, he wasn't sure where Binh Phu was, and it took him more than a week in Vietnam to find it. One of the first people he met on the path into the village was his cousin.

Thanh asked about his sister and learned she had survived the explosion that killed their mother and grandmother but was fatally wounded by artillery fire in an attack some months later.

"One leg was shot off from her body," Thanh's cousin said. "She was dying. We did what we could for her. The gunfire was too heavy to take her to a hospital. She begged, 'Please help me.' All we could do was sit there and watch. About eight that night we didn't hear her anymore. She died."

Distraught, Thanh walked deeper into Binh Phu, found the house where his aunt and uncle had once lived, and stood, weeping, in the front yard. From a window, his uncle recognized him.

"My uncle came running to me, and I to him, and we grabbed each other and cried a lot. That evening, practically everyone in the village came to listen to what had happened after I was taken away."

Thanh returned to Binh Phu from California three times after that 1980 trip, and on a recent visit, asked his aunts to choose him a wife. They chose a local woman, Thiet Nguyen, who was born after the war. She and Thanh spent some time together and agreed to the arranged marriage. We filmed the wedding yesterday in a nearby town.

Our guide's song of mourning is older than the American War, but the suffering it describes is timeless, universal. We reach the end of the trail, and he stops singing. There is no moon tonight, and the stars are hidden by clouds. It's so dark I can't see my hand in front of my face. We have trouble finding the car.

When I get home, I call John Balaban, who, as a conscientious objector, directed the American organization in Vietnam that saved Thanh's life. John is a poet and a professor of English. He helps choose *Thanh's War* as the title for our film and later sends me a poem.

FOR THE MISSING IN ACTION.
By John Balaban

Hazed with heat and harvest dust
the air swam with flying husks
as men whacked rice sheaves into bins
and all across the sunstruck fields
red flags hung from bamboo poles.
Beyond the last treeline on the horizon

Beyond the coconut palms and eucalyptus
out in the moon zone puckered by bombs
the dead earth where no one ventures,
the boys found it, foolish boys
riding buffaloes in craterlands
where at nights bombs thump and ghosts howl.
A green patch on the raw earth.
And now they've led the farmers here,
The kerchiefed women in baggy pants,
the men with sickles and flails, children
herding ducks with switches—all
staring from a crater berm; silent:
In that dead place the weeds had formed a man
where someone died and fertilized the earth, with flesh
and blood, with tears, with longing for loved ones.
No scrap remained; not even a buckle
survived the monsoons, just a green creature,
a viney man, supine, with posies for eyes,
butterflies for buttons, a lily for a tongue.
Now when huddled asleep together
the farmers hear a rustly footfall
as the leafman rises and stumbles to them.

THE TRAIN LURCHED back and forth several times before the engineer gave up and the motors stopped straining. My father and I sat in silence. He took me by the shoulders and turned me around so I was facing him. "We're not hurt," he said, looking directly into my eyes. "I believe the train is intact, but others may need help. We should find out."

He got up and gently pulled me along. I left Louie on the seat and stepped into the corridor, which had more light than our compartment. The windows on the north side of the train were only partly covered by snow. I saw that we were stuck above a fairly deep ravine.

Passengers stood in doorways, confused and afraid. One man joked, "Well, they promised us a trip we wouldn't forget!"

Like us, Sally and her parents had escaped injury, and they followed us forward through the train. In one car a man held a bloody towel to his head. He'd been hit by a suitcase knocked loose from the rack above his seat. In the lounge car, the conductor was trying to impose order among a fearful group. The lone doctor on the train, an elderly man accompanying a heart patient from Ohio, came to help, as did several nurses, including the woman whose lap Sally and I had fallen into our first day on the train. She tended someone who had fallen and sprained an ankle.

"From now on, this car is the clinic," the conductor said. "We're lucky. As far as we know, no one is seriously hurt and we're only temporarily stopped."

The Alaska-bound soldiers came into the lounge car in heavy coats and boots. They asked where they could be useful, and the conductor sent them outside to help trainmen assess the situation. "Be careful. The temperature is in the teens, and the wind is tearing limbs from trees."

"Should the rest of us shovel?" My father asked.

"Not yet. We have only a few shovels, and snow could slide again. Stay here and keep people calm. I'll come back later, but now I need to go forward to check on the engineer."

He left, and I went to a window to watch the soldiers struggle through drifts almost up to their waists.

I wondered if these events could really be happening, but instead of fear, I felt something like relief. Everyone around me was as confused and upset as I'd been for months. I wouldn't have to pretend anymore that everything was alright.

Is that what these obsessive memories are about? Am I most comfortable on the edge of loss?

Later our parents gave Sally and me permission to walk through the rest of the train, and we headed for the mystery car. Snow covered most windows. Some passengers made jokes. In one car, a group of men bet on our arrival time in Oakland. I could tell they were pretending not to be afraid. In another car, a woman strummed a ukulele. A porter came to reassure passengers that a giant snowplow called a rotary would soon free the train.

The door to the mystery car was still locked. We knocked hard and I yelled, "This is an emergency. Let us in!"

Inside—muffled voices. The door opened a crack, and the cowboy stuck his head out. "What did we hit?" His car had only the two small windows on the downhill side, and he didn't know what had happened.

"Ice and snow broke loose—an avalanche," I said as Sally and I pushed open the door. We were finally inside.

"What's your name?" I asked.

"I'm Fred Wyrick. This here is Jerry Stark."

Stark glowered from the end of the car. I saw his red shoes again and a plaid sport coat. I couldn't make sense of the two men. Who were they and why were they together when they seemed so different? And what was this car? The walls were paneled in knotty pine, like a rustic cabin. Rubber matting covered much of the floor. A wooden storage area, or a stall, took up part of the car, and next to it were bunk beds. I saw a camping stove and a small refrigerator at the other end.

I heard thumping again.

Thud! Bang! Someone or something was kicking a wall or the floor.

Suddenly, I knew. With a leap, I ran toward the stall and was about to enter when the cowboy grabbed me.

"He's frightened—move slowly."

Before me, tied with a rope to a brass ring, a large white stallion struggled to break free. The narrow space had kept him from falling when the avalanche hit, but now he pawed the floor in terror. I believed in the intelligence of animals and realized that his fear meant we were in more danger than I had thought, but I didn't care. He was magnificent, his coat thick and shining, white everywhere except for a black spot behind one ear. I felt an immediate connection to him, and to calm him down, I sang the first song that came to mind, the lullaby from "The Gunnywolf," a fairy tale: "Kum kwa kee wa, kum kwa kee wa." My mother had sung it when I was sick or frightened. The horse's ears turned forward, and he stopped straining at the rope. I entered the stall. Broad and tall, he seemed familiar.

I stepped back to take in all of him before turning to confront the two men.

"I watch *The Lone Ranger* every week on television mostly because of his horse, Silver. He was wild and got hurt. The Lone Ranger found him, healed his wounds, and then tried to set him free. Silver wouldn't go. This horse looks just like Silver. Did you steal the Lone Ranger's horse?"

At first the question stunned Fred Wyrick, but then he laughed out loud.

"No, we didn't steal Silver. But as you can see, this horse is very special. You must promise to keep him secret. Don't tell anyone that he's here."

The older guy, Jerry Stark, threatened to have the conductor throw us off the train if we talked about the horse, but Sally and I knew that wouldn't happen. From then on, we ignored Stark. For us, only Fred Wyrick and the horse mattered.

Sally joined me in the stall, and we stayed as close to the white stallion as we could, partly because he was warm and the car was cold. He was almost twice our height. At the farm back home, Flag and Penny seemed big, but this horse was huge.

We learned that his name was Sky, he belonged to Fred's uncle, and he was four years old.

"He weighs about 1,250 pounds," Fred said proudly, "and is a rodeo champion in Illinois, where I come from. He's famous there."

I found a brush and began grooming whatever part of the animal I could reach, trusting he wouldn't kick or step on me. When the sound of sliding snow made him nervous again, I sang, "Kum kwa kee wa, kum kwa kee wa." Sally brought a stool, and we took turns with the brush. Sky was clearly accustomed to attention from little girls. He seemed almost to purr as we cared for him.

When we finished, I turned back to the cowboy. "I don't understand why he has to be a secret, but we'll keep quiet as long as you'll allow us to visit him until we get to Oakland."

Fred looked at the other man, who frowned but nodded in agreement.

On the way back to the lounge car to check in with parents, we stopped to listen to the woman playing a uku-lele. A small group of passengers was singing "You Are My Sunshine." For some reason, the song made me cry. Sally took my hand.

"You know about my mother?"

"Your father told my parents."

In the lounge car/clinic, I listened as Daddy briefed other passengers. "The train is frozen in place," he said, "and we may not break free until tomorrow. To save batteries, the conductor wants us to go to bed when it gets dark. The first seating for dinner will begin at four-thirty."

Someone had removed most of the lounge chairs, and Sally's mother was helping the doctor treat people lying on blankets piled on the floor. The man whose suitcase had fallen on his head had a slight concussion. A woman was having heart fibrillations. Another passenger had a bronchial infection, which the doctor feared was turning into pneumonia. He had brought few medicines and said he would use gin to sterilize gauze and needles, if necessary.

Sally and I spent the rest of the afternoon reading to patients. After a light supper, Daddy and I went to bed, but I lay awake worrying about Sky. What would happen to him if the train remained stranded for long? Did he have enough food? Was he getting exercise? How long could a horse stand being cooped up in a train?

CHILE — 2004

During long days of shooting in Santiago, I almost miss a story central to our film.

Codirector Patricio Lanfranco and I have been following Judge Juan Guzmán with a camera crew as he investigates charges of murder against Augusto Pinochet. (In Chile, judges both investigate and try cases.) On this day we're filming the judge's meeting at Santiago police headquarters with a group of women who are witnesses in a case involving many victims. In late 1974, a year after General Pinochet overthrew President Salvador Allende, security forces abducted, tortured, and "disappeared" the children of these women. Members of the revolutionary group MIR, they had resisted the coup and were in hiding when taken.

The mothers were suspicious of Judge Guzmán at first because they knew he had supported General Pinochet. The judge's father was a well-known diplomat/poet, and the Guzmán family was historically conservative. Believing that Allende's nationalizations and land reform went too far, Judge Guzmán had supported the violent coup led by Pinochet, who promised order in Chile again. Guzmán said that he had considered early reports of torture and assassination by Pinochet's forces "communist propaganda."

As a judge of the Santiago Court of Appeals, Guzmán was randomly appointed to investigate the first charges of murder and kidnapping against Pinochet, and though he could have refused, he recognized that this was the defining moment of his life and accepted the assignment. After many months of work, he has won the trust of the women in this room by uncovering and publicizing new evidence in cases involving their children and many other victims.

Bodyguards accompany him wherever he goes because of assassination threats from Pinochet supporters.

We get a compression shot of Guzmán walking down a long hall toward us, an elegant sixty-five-year-old man flanked by young police detectives from a special investigative unit funded by the democratically elected Chilean government. Pinochet was forced out of office by a pro-democracy movement some years ago. The judge and detectives take seats in front of the room behind a long table.

"Thank you very much for coming," Guzmán says.

"Oh no," the women respond in unison, "Thank *you!*"

I study them. One is at least ninety and bent by arthritis. Others are in their early to mid-eighties and seem in good health. They are white-haired, friendly, garrulous. They've known one another for a long time. If alive now, their children would be about sixty, my age. They were abducted and disappeared at about the same time as Jorge Müller, my cameraman friend from 1970. The women knew Jorge's mother, who died several years ago, and they also know his father, whom I visited earlier on this trip.

I feel close to Jorge just being in this room.

Judge Guzmán says, "I want to ask those of you who have already testified to expand on your police statements. And I need your habeas corpus petitions. I don't know if you have them, but I need them urgently."

The mothers nod, "Sí, Sí." Chile had been democratic for decades before the coup, and during Pinochet's fierce repression, mothers like these filed habeas corpus petitions, which, if granted, would have forced the secret police to present their children in court and justify their arrests. More than ten thousand habeas corpus petitions were filed in Chile after the coup; all were denied. Some judges were too frightened to do anything else; others supported the violent repression of the Left as a necessary evil.

I think of my own children and grandchildren. These women have spent much of their lives trying to discover what happened to a beloved son or daughter. A few of the mothers seem broken, but others are vibrant, playful. The return of democracy to Chile happened partly because of their relentless search for the truth and their demand for justice.

The next day, Patricio and I interview several of the mothers in a small apartment in an old neighborhood across from the Santiago Racetrack. Each one tells a story difficult to hear. I am tired by the time Edita Salvadores de Castro, age seventy-four, begins:

"On November 17, 1974, at about two in the morning, they came to our house and detained my husband and me. My husband could see from under the blindfold, and he knew they took us to Jose Domingo Cañas, a house they used for detention.

"There they threatened me, saying that if we didn't tell them where Chechi and my son-in-law Juan Carlos were—Chechi is what we called my daughter—they would kill my granddaughter. Chechi and Juan Carlos had a little girl, who at that time was a year and nine months old.

"What do I do? We knew they were surrounded, and we had to save the little girl.

"I said to my husband, Angel, 'Chechi would never forgive me for as long as we live . . . never . . . Because she told me, Mama, my daughter is for you. You raise her if something happens to me and Juan Carlos.'"

"So we took them to where they were, which was nearby.

"They gave us the child and detained Juan Carlos and Chechi right in front of us."

I hear every word, but it seems Edita is speaking a language other than Spanish, which I understand. Patricio is on the telephone during the interview and misses what she said.

Now, three days later, in my San Francisco office, I have finished transcribing the tape.

Edita and her husband led the police to her daughter's apartment. In return, Valentina, the granddaughter, survived.

ON THE FOURTH day of our trip on the train, I woke up very cold and, at Daddy's urging, put on two layers of clothing under my coat. We went to the dining car for the latest news. Conditions had worsened. The blizzard continued, and snow now covered most of the streamliner. Only a few downhill windows were clear. The air was foul. Lights flickered. Cars were cold and mostly dark.

In the dining car, the conductor briefed passengers. He said that an avalanche had hit two large plows trying to help us. They derailed, and an engineer on one of the plows was killed when it toppled over. The conductor seemed on the

verge of tears. He said a locomotive had reached us in the night to supply steam heat, but a valve had frozen open and the water supply for that engine had run out.

Someone asked why snow couldn't be melted to replace the water and was told it was too cold to melt snow in something called a tender. The crew had already tried and failed. Electrical batteries that powered lights were running down and couldn't be recharged.

Our train would soon be freezing cold and dark.

Some brave people had gotten through from nearby Crystal Springs to say help was coming. A dog sled with food and medicines would arrive by dark.

The doctor stepped forward to explain that the head steward would ration the remaining food. Milk was available only for children under ten. There wouldn't be much to eat until more provisions arrived, but no one would starve.

There was enough drinking water in tanks for two or three days.

Passengers should do whatever they could to stay warm. Curtains and bedding could be torn up and used for wrapping bodies and especially feet. Anything in the train made of wood should be brought into the dining car to be burned for cooking and heat. As an example, the conductor mentioned the trays that passengers used for card-playing. He told people to rotate through the diner every couple of hours to get warm. Alcoholic beverages were forbidden and smoking permitted only in vestibules.

I listened, fascinated. Some bathrooms weren't working, and the train had poor ventilation.

Vestibule doors would be cleared by shoveling and would be opened for five minutes each hour to keep air circulating. More crews would arrive soon from Crystal Springs. They were hiking in.

Someone asked how they could get in when we couldn't get out. The conductor explained that the men from Crystal Springs were risking burial by another avalanche.

For now, we were safer inside the train than out.

Our fathers left with axes to break up Pullman car ladders and wooden racks in the baggage car for the fire in the galley of the dining car. Sally's mother continued to help the doctor. She made us promise to stay inside the train, but we were free to go where we wanted.

In the mystery car, the door was open, and we went straight to the horse and embraced him. He submitted to my petting, nuzzling my hair and nibbling gently at a barrette. His naughtiness made us laugh.

"He doesn't mind the cold," Fred said. "He spent every day in the winter outside at my uncle's farm. We never coddled him."

Fred stood in the doorway of the stall, watching us.

"Why do you live on your uncle's farm?" I asked.

"My father was killed during the war, and my mother died a couple of years after that. I've lived with my uncle ever since. Where is your mother?"

The question startled me, but at least I could answer, "She died not long ago." Then I changed the subject.

"Where are you taking Sky?"

"To a trainer near San Francisco."

"Why?"

He didn't respond but came into the stall, picked up Sky's blanket, and took it into the vestibule, where he shook it out an open window. Sally and I brushed the horse from one end to the other and then did it again. I saw a narrow trough in the floor along the wall with a drain for hosing out urine and manure.

A small bucket of oats hung near the stall—"enough for today," Fred said. "The conductor has promised to try to get more, but rescue crews shouldn't have to take risks for a horse. If we're stranded beyond tonight and no food arrives, I'll have to ride Sky back to Norden—or try to walk by myself. I'm told I can get oats at a ranch on this side of the town that has pack horses."

Jerry Stark snarled from a corner. "My guy in Detroit paid a fortune for that horse, kid. You can forget about taking him out in this blizzard. "

Later, Fred said he was going to lead his horse on a walk in the car for exercise. "It will be better than nothing."

"I'll ride him bareback," I said. "We have a horse at home."

"It's too risky. If snow slides and he stumbles, he'd crush you."

"He needs me on his back to feel useful. Please let me try."

Fred bridled his horse and called me over, clasping his hands together so I could swing high onto Sky's back. We barely fit in the available space, and the horse walked gingerly, almost bending himself in half on each turn. I leaned as far forward as I could to avoid hitting the ceiling.

To keep the car from getting too cold, Fred smashed a chair and fed it piece by piece into a fire in a metal trash container. Doors at both ends stayed open for ventilation. Under me, Sky felt like a furnace, and his breath left a trail of steam behind us as we turned in the cold air. Looking around, I was filled with a sense of wonder so powerful that it almost drove out my shame and sorrow.

CHILE — 2006

We film Edita reading a poem by the Spaniard José Agustín Goytisolo, a gift from Chechi not long before she and her husband were captured. It's late afternoon on a warm spring day. Edita stands on her deck in light that's changing from bright to burnished gold.

> *You can't turn back*
> *because life thrusts you forward*
> *like a wave*
> *rolling, rolling.*
> *You will feel hemmed in*
> *lost and alone*
> *You may wish you'd never been born,*
> *but remember always what I wrote,*
> *thinking of you*
> *as I am now.*

Life is Beautiful.
You will see that in spite of sorrows,
you will have friends.
You will have love.
You will have friends.

Edita's granddaughter Valentina, now thirty-two years old, refuses to be interviewed on camera, but today she brings her baby boy to her grandparents' house and allows us to film them together. Edita and Angel are the only parents Valentina remembers, and their mutual affection is evident as they tease and hug each other. Valentina is married to a Spaniard and serves as director of public relations for a European organization that owns one of the world's most advanced optical instruments, a huge telescope in the Atacama Desert.

Valentina's aunt, who was abducted the same day as Chechi and Juan Carlos, told us that Osvaldo Romo, an infamously sadistic member of the security force known as DINA, was in charge of questioning the three of them at Jose Domingo Cañas, a torture center. DINA tried to break people before their comrades could find new hiding places, and Valentina's father didn't survive for long. A prisoner released later said he heard a torturer shout, "Shit, you killed him before he could talk."

Chechi was moved from the torture house to Villa Grimaldi, a concentration camp, where Juan Carlos's sister was also briefly imprisoned. When the sister was released, Chechi told her good-bye and said, "Kiss my parents for me, and tell Valentina that I love her."

When and where Chechi died remains a mystery. She may have been among hundreds of prisoners tied to pieces of railroad tracks and dumped from army helicopters into the Pacific Ocean. My friend Jorge Müller almost certainly died that way. I imagine him and Chechi lying side by side at the bottom of Quintero Bay as every trace of them disappears. A scuba diver found pieces of rail in the bay, and we filmed him bringing them to the surface under the supervision of Judge Guzmán.

Affixed by rust to a rail was a button later found by experts to be made of *nácar*, mother of pearl, a ring of white fire seared into my mind.

RIELES
DE LA
MUERTE

NEW YORK — FEBRUARY 2001

Over the past two years, the Clinton administration has released more than twenty-four thousand formerly classified US documents that contain significant evidence of US efforts to undermine Salvador Allende, destroy democracy in Chile, and bolster General Augusto Pinochet. Some of the information was available because of a congressional investigation in the 1970s, but reading the documents themselves is chilling.

Memorandum for the Record: 16 September 1970

From: William V. Broe, Chief, Western Hemisphere Division, Central Intelligence Agency . . .

The Director told the group that President Nixon had decided that an Allende regime in Chile was not acceptable to the United States. The President asked the Agency to prevent Allende from coming to power or to unseat him. The President authorized ten million dollars for this purpose.

Henry Kissinger oversaw US policy toward Chile as national security advisor and then a secretary of state between 1969 and 1977. He has agreed to discuss the document release. On the morning of the interview, in his office in New York, he tells producer Mary Jo Brooks and me that he doesn't want to talk about the content of the documents but only the broader issue of whether secret cables and memoranda "to and from the field" about covert operations should ever be released at all. He thinks they shouldn't because of "the ease with which they lend themselves to distortion."

I tell him the issue of declassification of these papers is inseparable from their content. The documents are important because of what's in them. He cajoles Mary Jo and me, alternately praising *The NewsHour* and instructing us how to do our work. "Don't take me out of context," he says. "I can't cover these subjects in a short time."

Strangely, as filming begins, I'm not nervous. There is one question in particular I have long wanted to ask, and he answers it. It's a longer question than Jim Lehrer would approve.

ELIZABETH FARNSWORTH: *Let's look at Pinochet's situation. He's charged [in Chile] with fifty-seven murders and eighteen kidnappings perpetrated as part of one particular case that's called the Caravan of Death. You met with him face to face in 1976.*

One of the things the documents show is that in this conversation you brought up human rights, but you also told him, "We are behind you; we are sympathetic with what you're trying to do here. I think the previous government was headed toward communism. I think you are a victim of the left wing groups around the world."

Why did you not say to him: "You're violating human rights? You're killing people. Stop it?"

HENRY KISSINGER: *First of all, human rights were not an international issue at the time, the way they have become since . . .*

But it was also true that we were convinced as I said, as you correctly quoted, I was convinced that Allende was heading the country toward communism. At that time, Argentina was in chaos. Uruguay had a radical left-wing revolution. Peru had a left-wing socialist military government. And Castro was still a vital force. So we believed that the establishment of a Castro-like regime in Chile would create a sequence of events in all of the, in

least the southern cone of Latin America—it would
be extremely inimical to the national interests of
the United States at a time when the Cold War was
at its height. And for that reason, we did not want
to weaken Pinochet to a point where the Allende
people would come back.

I also ask about the US role in the botched kidnapping of army chief of staff General René Schneider. Kissinger concedes that the CIA sent guns for the kidnapping but says he personally called off the operation several days before it happened. The plotters went ahead and did it on their own, he claims. I remind him that a recent special CIA report to Congress about covert operations in Chile confirms that the agency paid Schneider's assassins hush money *after* the killing. Kissinger responds, "This is exactly what I didn't want to do, because thirty years after, there is no possible way I can remember."

The assassination of General René Schneider was a direct result of US-funded efforts to instigate a military coup in the days before Allende was inaugurated as president. Those who ended up killing Schneider had CIA support, and the agency paid them afterward to keep quiet and helped them relocate outside the country.

AFTER WATCHING ME ride Sky for a while, Sally got on too, and we rode back and forth, giggling as if we weren't on a horse's back in a freezing train, stuck in a mountain blizzard. Sky pranced from time to time, and it felt like dancing.

"Quit horsing around," Fred said, and we all laughed. "The last thing we need is for him to bolt." He pointed to workers shoveling outside the train. They'd noticed us but didn't find a horse in a fancy car surprising. They'd seen it before.

At noon, Sally's mother came looking for us with sandwiches and was shocked by what she found—two girls in a freezing train car on a horse whose coat glowed red from the fire. She stopped and rubbed her eyes twice before coming farther, and at first she was furious.

"You should have told me about this, Sally! You're riding a horse in a train car. It's dangerous!"

Fred stepped up and spoke with authority. "The girls are keeping him from going stir crazy," he said. "Please don't punish them. They're a big help to the horse and to me."

The other man also tried to smooth things over. He explained that the horse was headed for a trainer near San

Francisco and mentioned something about Hollywood. I didn't think he was lying, but he wasn't telling the whole truth.

While he and Sally's mother talked, I whispered to Fred about the dog sled expected in the night. "Maybe they can take you to Norden. We'll take care of Sky if you're not back by morning."

Later that afternoon, I walked alone back through the dark train. All was quiet; everyone's gears seemed to have wound down, like Tik-tok. The darkness frightened and also interested me. As I groped my way through a chair car, a conductor appeared with a kerosene lantern, and I saw people huddled together in their seats for warmth. They'd wrapped themselves in whatever they could find—coats, blankets, curtains. A few people complained—one even threatened to sue—but mostly they just wanted to know when we might be rescued. One person compared us to something called the Donner Party. I didn't know what he meant.

I was impressed to see how well people coped. The conductor stopped and spoke quietly to some passengers. When he saw me, he said that a section crew had risked their lives to pull two propane-fueled generators on sleds from Crystal Springs. Two sleeping cars would have light tonight, and ours was one of them. Anyone with children would sleep in those cars, but families had to double up. Sally and her parents would share our compartment with my father and me.

After an early dinner of one hot dog, Jell-O, and potato chips, we gathered in our bedroom and stood awkwardly in the small space discussing who should sleep where. Finally, Sally, her mother, and I took the top berth, and the men shared the bottom. We kept our clothes on for warmth but were still cold.

Teeth chattering, I read from *The Road to Oz*. Dorothy continued her journey toward the Emerald City with four companions besides Tik-tok: a shaggy man; a chicken named Billina; a boy named Button-Bright; and Polychrome, the rainbow's daughter.

They proceeded on their journey in a friendly group
for Polychrome had discovered that the copper
man was harmless and was no longer afraid of him.
Button-Bright was also reassured, and took quite
a fancy to Tik-tok. He wanted the clockwork man
to open himself, so that he might see the wheels go
round; but that was a thing Tik-tok could not do.
Button-Bright then wanted to wind up the copper
man, and Dorothy promised he should do so as soon
as any part of the machinery ran down. This pleased

Button-Bright, who held fast to one of Tik-tok's
copper hands as he trudged along the road, while
Dorothy walked on the other side of her old friend
and Billina perched by turns upon his shoulder or
his copper hat. Polly once more joyously danced
ahead and Toto ran after her, barking with glee. The
shaggy man was left to walk behind; but he didn't
seem to mind that a bit, and whistled merrily or
looked curiously upon the pretty scenes they passed.

I put the book down and thought about what I'd read and the experiences of the afternoon. Like Dorothy, I was on a journey and had faced danger and observed "pretty scenes" with my companions. I had talked more with Fred that afternoon. He said he had accompanied Sky on the train from Illinois to keep him calm but would return to his uncle's farm as soon as possible from Oakland. Fred admitted that he was sad and would miss his beautiful horse.

I thought we had much in common.

I started to read the book aloud again and then felt queasy, sick to my stomach. The air seemed heavy. I tried to sit up but couldn't even raise my head. I remembered the poppies in *The Wizard of Oz* that put Dorothy and her friends to sleep. Sally and her mother were too quiet. No one had said good night. I cried for help, and then I was falling, tumbling through darkness that reached beyond forever.

TOPEKA—1957

After a disagreement with my stepmother, I couldn't sleep and got out of bed to watch a late-night movie about World War II on television. Two years before my father had married a widow with a very large house. Marcia was at college, and my parents and three step-siblings were asleep. My new sisters and brother were younger. I liked them very much but hadn't yet adjusted to having a stepmother. At night, I sought relief in movies. The house was so big that no one could hear me. I don't remember what I saw that night, but it must have introduced me to the Holocaust.

The next morning I asked my father, "Where were the good Germans? Why didn't they prevent those terrible things from happening?"

"Are you learning about this in school?"

I didn't want him to know I stayed up late at night watching television, so I said yes. "It's hard to talk about this over breakfast, Elizabeth," he told me, "and I don't have a quick answer. There was resistance from good Germans to the Nazis, but not enough. The Nazis had the guns. We'll discuss it later."

"ELIZABETH, CAN YOU hear me?"

I opened my eyes and saw my father and the doctor in a halo of light cast by a lantern. They kneeled beside me in the lounge-car clinic, where I lay on blankets folded on the floor. Carbon monoxide from the emergency generators had poisoned us, the doctor said. A nurse had smelled the gas while walking through our car. She ran to get James Dodge, and he and other porters broke into sleeping compartments and saved many lives. Sally waved at me from across the aisle. The doctor went to examine her.

I whispered to my father, "I want Mommy here. I want her so very much."

He took my hand and held it.

We slept in the clinic the rest of the night and felt better the next morning. After toast and cocoa in the dining

car, the only warm car on the train, we went into a vestibule, where the window was open for ventilation. Snow fell lightly and the fierce wind had stopped. About forty men in heavy green coats were shoveling a wide path alongside the train. I saw a small fire where several of the men were warming their hands.

As we watched, Fred Wyrick came running into the vestibule. He said he had been looking for us.

"Are you alright? I heard what happened."

During the night, he'd gone to Norden on snowshoes with volunteers after they'd delivered emergency food and medicine to the train on a dog sled.

"I got oats for Sky and came back with the sled this morning. Sky is frantic to go outside. We can't hide him anymore without endangering his life. Are you well enough to help?"

My father didn't hesitate. "I'll come."

I felt stronger with each breath. "I'll do what I can."

In his car Sky snorted and pulled on his rope. He was more nervous than I'd seen him before, and I caressed and sang to him while my father and Jerry opened the sliding door and unfolded a ramp, placing it between the doorway and the shoveled path. The ramp was narrow; if the horse shied, he'd fall. Fred brought him from the stall and handed me the reins. I walked him back and forth in the car, singing "Kum kwa kee wa, kum kwa kee wa."

"Look outside," I sang. "See the path they've shoveled? *Hush shhhh, shhh.*" His breathing slowed. Fred led him to the door and stepped onto the ramp, but Sky wouldn't follow. I pushed from behind. Reluctantly, he moved one foot forward and then another. When he reached the path, he took deep breaths and stood tall, looking around and up at the light snow. He was white against white, perfection in a broken world. I could see fallen branches and, near the train, the snow plow where the engineer had been killed. The section hands stopped working to watch. Windows filled with passengers, including Sally and her parents. Putting his hands together, Daddy helped Fred and me onto Sky's back. On the first step, his right foreleg went deep in a drift. Snorting in frustration, he pulled it out and kept going. After that, the path was more packed. His ears turned forward, and he whinnied, thanking us for his liberation.

Inside the train, passengers cheered. Some wept at the sight.

We rode Sky past mail and baggage cars to the locomotive, where the engineer leaned out, clapping and cheering. Then we rode back the other way. We did that again and again. Passengers came out to watch, and Fred let them pat his horse. No one asked who Sky was or why he was there. He was a blessing that needed no explanation.

After several hours outside, Fred leaned back on the horse and whispered to me, "I have something important to say. You were right."

"What about?"

"Sky resembling Silver. You're sitting on the Lone Ranger's next horse. Jerry's boss in Detroit owns the Lone Ranger radio and television programs. He bought Sky from my uncle with money that will pay for my college education. The current Silver is too old for the tricks required by the show, but his fans are loyal and might reject a substitute. We can't tell anyone that Sky is his replacement."

He added, "We'll be rescued at first light tomorrow, before anyone else."

I was too stunned to speak.

Later, Fred and I dismounted and led Sky back up the ramp. He went willingly into his stall.

"Highway 40 will be cleared by morning," Fred said. The trainer is coming to get us. I hope you'll say good-bye."

MY FATHER AND I awoke at daybreak on our sixth day on the train. It had finally stopped snowing. We went straight to the horse car, where my father and Fred unfolded the ramp and set it up again. Fred led Sky down. I didn't have to push this time.

The path now reached about a quarter of a mile down to Highway 40, where a truck and horse trailer waited. I saw a man and the glow of his cigarette beside the truck.

I could tell Fred was relieved to free Sky from his prison, but this was their last day together. The conflicting emotions rendered him almost mute.

Sky lowered his head when I whispered, "Good-bye, my beautiful friend. Good-bye."

Daddy rubbed his ears. "We'll be watching you, big guy. Good luck."

The conductor, two brakemen, and James Dodge came out of the train. The men shook hands, and then Fred leaned down to hug me. I was shaking, partly from the cold, and he held me for a moment but didn't linger. Turning, he led Sky down the path. I started to follow, but my father put his arm around me to keep me back.

The man by the truck met them and took the reins. Sky raised his head and whinnied, a cry that filled me with both joy and sorrow. I didn't know until then that they could be felt at the same time. Then Sky walked up the ramp into the van. A minute later he was gone.

That afternoon, my father, Sally, her parents, and I trudged with more than two hundred passengers and crew down the path to trucks and cars provided by volunteers who lived along Highway 40. Almost everyone was wrapped in blankets or curtains. For many hours, the volunteer drivers ferried us to another train about five miles to the west. During the five-hour trip to Oakland, doctors treated passengers who were ill, and everyone got a free steak or any meal they wanted. Even after dark, people came out along the tracks to cheer the rescue train. Once the blizzard let up, news photographers in airplanes and helicopters got pictures and film of what they were calling "the stranded streamliner." We had become big news throughout the country.

When Sally and I parted in Oakland in the middle of the night, we cried and promised to write each other. My father and I took a ferry under the Bay Bridge to San Francisco. In our hotel room high on a hill, I looked for *The Road to Oz* to read myself to sleep, but I had left it on the train.

PART II

A FTER TWO RAINY days of sightseeing in San Francisco, my father and I boarded the Coast Daylight for Santa Barbara, where my great-aunt and -uncle owned a lemon orchard. We had planned our trip mainly to visit them in the warmth of southern California, and I was glad to be on our way again. I felt no fear when the train's engines revved, the whistle blew, and wheels began to turn. What had happened before seemed like a dream.

As we pulled out of the city, I held Louie up to the window to watch. I liked San Francisco and wanted him to see more of California.

In Palo Alto, my father talked about Stanford University, where an uncle had studied. As we approached Salinas, I saw advertisements for artichokes and asked my father if he liked them. He said he'd never tried one. After that he pointed out vast fields covered with straw to protect what he thought were strawberries or flowers.

Later in the day, the train climbed up to San Luis Obispo and then down into valleys verdant from the same storm that had stranded us in the Sierra. We traveled southwest until the Pacific Ocean stretched before us to the horizon. When the tracks turned south, we sped for many miles alongside the sea, immense and mysterious like the Kansas prairie.

Off a wide beach I saw a boy floating on a long board beyond breaking waves.

"What's he doing?"

"It's called surfing."

Fascinated, I watched as he paddled to catch a swelling of the sea. As the wave formed, he rose with it. When he stood up on the board, I saw that he wasn't much older than I was. He rode the crest of the wave ahead of the break, parallel with our train. When the water crashed down, he dropped through the air, and I gasped in fear. But he caught the inside curve and rode even farther. I could barely see him through the spray. As we pulled ahead, he dove and disappeared, his board skipping behind him. I imagined myself in his wake, moving almost as fast as a train.

As we drew close to Santa Barbara, the sun dropped toward the horizon. We skirted lemon and orange groves, where light flashed like fire through the trees.

We had come a long way from Kansas and the frozen Sierra. At the station I felt like Dorothy after the tornado, opening the door to Oz.

THE FIRST MORNING at their home in Montecito, on the edge of Santa Barbara, Aunt Betty served homemade doughnuts and hot chocolate for breakfast. She sat at the end of a shiny wooden table with me and my father on either side. Crystal glasses on the table sparkled in the early light. Uncle Bob had already gone into the orchard, and from the dining room window I could see him among the trees. Beyond were high hills, home to the coyotes I had heard in the night.

As we talked, a grandfather clock in the living room chimed the early hour. Before breakfast I had climbed onto a stool and opened tiny doors to inspect the clock's chimes and moon dial. In my bedroom drawer, I'd discovered a new yellow blouse and golden barrettes wrapped in bright blue paper. I was wearing the barrettes now. Aunt Betty allowed me as many doughnuts as I wanted and said I could dip them in the hot chocolate. I felt enveloped in her warmth.

Though she and Uncle Bob visited Topeka at least once a year, I didn't know them well. On the train from San Francisco, Daddy had talked about the lives of his aunt and his mother, my grandmother.

"Aunt Betty is two years younger than Mother," he said. "Their father deserted the family when the girls were young, and they had to quit school and go to work. They sometimes went to bed hungry. When I was young, we prayed with Mother every night for hungry children."

From the beginning I felt closely observed by Aunt Betty. On the second day we adopted a schedule, and its predictability was soothing. In the morning we weeded outdoor flower and vegetable beds and tended orchids in the greenhouse. In the afternoon we made fresh doughnuts or gathered shells on a nearby beach. After dinner we turned the shells into jewelry for cousins and friends in Topeka.

On the fifth night in Montecito, the earth shook, frightening me, and I cried for my mother. Aunt Betty came running and sat on the side of the bed, cradling me in her arms. When Daddy came to help, she motioned for him to leave.

"It was an earthquake, darling," she said. We have them sometimes."

I was sobbing, catching my breath, and then crying again.

"I imagine you miss her very much," she said. I knew she wanted me to talk about Mother, and I was grateful for her sympathy and affection, but I couldn't find the words yet.

The next morning I got up before anyone else and went exploring.

IRAQ — MAY 2003

The crew and I watch from the second floor of a building in Basra as people's lives float out the windows. Looters have taken everything: doorknobs, file cabinets, desks, chairs, doors, windowpanes. Only papers remain, and they're drifting in the desert wind.

Our fixer, Fakher Haider, a tall, soft-spoken Iraqi, grabs a document before it disappears—someone's birth certificate, he says. We each (correspondent, producer, two cameramen, and a soundman) join in snatching pages out of the air and then sit on the floor as Fakher translates. We had hired him on the advice of a UN official when we arrived just after the US invasion. Now he reads to us from deeds and business licenses.

"This is the central records repository of the Basra governorate," he explains. "Legal documents were stored here."

Our work is more dangerous than I anticipated, and we're more than usually dependent on our fixer. Fakher was managing a fertilizer factory when the war started. Now he interprets for us, schedules interviews, gathers information, and works to keep us safe. Years of psychopathic

dictatorship, warfare, economic embargo, and US bombing—plus the invasion and subsequent looting—have taken
a terrible toll on Iraq, and I use the word *apocalyptic* when
describing the situation to executive producer Les Crystal at
The NewsHour back home.

The sixth angel of the apocalypse has emptied his vial
into the Euphrates, and post-invasion Iraq is the result.

One of the cameramen spent part of last night in the hotel
bathtub because of a gunfight just outside. I use earplugs
and didn't hear the noise, but none of us has gotten much
sleep in the weeks since we arrived. We work warily because
of the hostility we sense wherever we go. American and
other troops have liberated Shiites from Saddam Hussein,
but the cost—in lives and damage to infrastructure—is very
high. Shiites and Sunnis alike are suffering from destruction
caused by the invasion. When I talk to someone in the street,
Fakher translates. Sometimes in the middle of the interview,
he says quietly, in English, "We must leave *now*." Later
he would explain that he'd heard, or sensed, a threat from
someone in the crowd.

We film at the Basra waterworks, where looters have
stolen the motors from four multimillion-dollar pumps.
They are large pieces of machinery, so the thieves must have
arrived with trucks and cranes. The First Battalion of the

Duke of Wellington's Regiment, which is responsible for post-invasion Basra, had control of the city when it was happening but did little to stop the looting. It's not their mandate, they claim, and anyway they don't have enough troops. Later we film children drinking from the pipes, broken now, that had carried dirty water to the looted purification plant. In a hospital, we interview a doctor treating children with cholera. Exploring the town, we come upon the ruins of a house where a dazed man is lifting heavy pieces of rubble. After welcoming us to shoot video of what remains of his home, Mr. Al Raimahai asks to borrow my satellite phone so he can inform relatives in London that his wife, daughters, uncle, niece, and nephew have been killed by an American bomb meant for the house next door, wrongly believed to belong to one of Saddam Hussein's generals, according to Mr. Raimahai. He had survived because he left home early that day to guard his business. He welcomes us, apologizing for not being able to offer tea, and leads us silently through what used to be his home, "collateral damage" in an invasion some people back home are calling a success.

I talk with Fakher but never learn whether he's glad or angry about the US invasion. Perhaps he hasn't decided yet. He is Shi'a and was tortured in prison under Saddam

Hussein. He had joined a sniper brigade in the Shi'a uprising that followed the Gulf War. He says the religious leaders of that uprising deserted their followers and escaped to Iran and other places. Tens of thousands of fighters like Fakher were killed during the uprising by the forces of Saddam Hussein, and Fakher narrowly avoided death himself.

Now his former Shi'a commanders have returned. "Nothing good can come of rule by them," Fakher says.

He is poor and thin but very strong. With his help, we shoot a huge outdoor rally in honor of Ayatollah Muhammad Bakr al-Hakim on the day he returns from Iran. I had interviewed the ayatollah several months earlier in Tehran, where he lived in exile after the 1991 Shi'a uprising in Iraq. Because they recognize me, his people invite me and producer Scott Tong to stand on stage at the rally while cameraman Brian Gill and Fakher shoot from below. Thousands of people pour onto the field as the ayatollah arrives in a convoy from Iran, and Brian, a big man with a heavy video camera, gets crushed by the crowd. He yells, "I can't breathe." Fakher pushes him to the front and boosts him onto the stage. From then on, they call each other brother, and Brian tells everyone he meets that Fakher saved his life.

JUST AFTER DAWN, I ran down the steep steps of my
aunt's house to an unpaved driveway where a barely visible
path began. I had spotted it the day before and asked Aunt
Betty where it went. She thought it might be an old horse
path from Santa Barbara through Montecito but didn't
know where it ended. I ran down the path, hardly notic-
ing what was around me, and stopped when it ended at a
driveway made of large, flat stones that led to the left up
a rise toward higher hills. Eucalyptus trees with drooping
branches lined the way as I ran upward until the stones ran
out.

Before me was a three-story white house with a red tile
roof, iron grilles over the windows, and a large front door,
which was open. Workers were unloading lights and other
equipment from a truck, and I followed them into the house
and down the corridor to a large room with thick beams and
a wooden table and couch seemingly made for giants.

Across from the doorway, a woman stood in the light
of a floor-to-ceiling window, reading aloud. I watched for a
few moments and then sat down in the corner. She had light

curly hair and wore a straight blue skirt, white blouse, and high heels.

I see now that she dressed like my mother.

Speaking with just the slightest accent, she read the same sentence repeatedly, emphasizing it differently each time. Perhaps she was foreign, but she might as well have been from a different planet, so unusual was this scene in my eyes.

"There was someone in this house," she read. "Something violent happened."

First she read quietly, as if too nervous to speak. Then she read louder and faster, as if spitting out the words. She was testing which way was better.

After that she looked around and noticed me in the corner.

"An interloper! How impolite! Introduce yourself."

"I'm Elizabeth from Topeka, I said, pointing. "Over there is the house of my aunt and uncle."

"I don't know them. We're using this place to shoot a movie."

She was coming straight at me, speaking sharply.

"You can't just waltz onto a film set."

I jumped up, ready to bolt, but something made her stop. I saw her body soften. She moved back a few steps and kneeled down.

"If you're quiet, you may stay for a while, but if you interrupt us even once, I'll send you back out."

And then, *clack, clack, clack* on her high heels, she returned to the window and read again from the pages in her hand.

"She never left this house. Something terrible happened to her."

I watched as other members of the cast and crew came in, including a tall, handsome man. He and the beautiful woman practiced while cameras and lights were adjusted, and then the actors got made up, which took a while. When they were ready, the man in charge called, "Action." The actress stopped the filming when she didn't like how it was going, and the director—I guess that's what he was—took her advice.

What I sensed in the room seemed familiar to me, as if I'd been there before.

The actors were portraying fear, dread, and shame. I had those feelings myself and was surprised they could be performed. The experience made me feel less strange.

By the time they finished the scene, it was early afternoon. Aunt Betty appeared in the doorway, out of breath, concerned. She realized what had happened, apologized, and took me firmly by the hand.

As we left, the actress, who never told me her name, called out, "We needed an audience today, Elizabeth from Topeka. Wherever you were headed, I'm glad you ended up here."

Walking back on the path, my aunt pulled me along. Peeved, she was deciding if punishment should follow.

After a few minutes, she said,

"That was Ida Lupino, darling, and her husband, Howard Duff. She's one of the most famous stars in Hollywood. You're lucky they allowed you to watch."

That night, when she put me to bed, my aunt talked about herself.

"I was in eighth grade when my father went away. Mother said he'd been sent to Albuquerque by the Santa Fe, and I think he worked there for a while, but when he came back to Topeka, he lived with another woman. I saw them downtown together one day. Why didn't he come to visit us—his daughters? Did my mother refuse permission to visit? I never asked and will never know. I longed for him, but eventually his loss no longer defined my life. The same thing will happen to you, Elizabeth."

"But your father was *alive*. There was a chance he'd come back."

"Well, that's true, darling. Your mother can't return. But you have the rest of us. I'll visit more often. You have two grandmothers, four aunts, a sister, and your father in Topeka. You won't feel alone."

I thought about what she was saying.

"I guess you could say we have good bad luck. Sweet dreams, Aunt Betty."

The next morning I got up early again and walked the overgrown path to the mansion. I saw the same trucks and film equipment, but the front door was locked, and when I rang the bell, no one answered. I sat on the front veranda, hoping to see Ida Lupino, but she never came out. After that, my aunt and I followed our daily routine. When our eight-day visit ended, she and Uncle Bob took me and my father to Los Angeles, where we boarded another train, the Golden State Limited, which took a southern route to Topeka. I missed Sally on the return trip and made no new friends. In Barstow, Winslow, and Albuquerque, I got out of the train to walk up and down the platform. Sometimes I searched for my mother. I hadn't given up all hope of seeing her again.

At home in Topeka, I told Marcia about Sally, the train ride, San Francisco, and Ida Lupino. I didn't mention Sky or being stranded in a blizzard.

I said that Aunt Betty lived in a place more beautiful than Oz.

"She grows flowers called birds of paradise. Mother would love them, don't you think?"

BERKELEY—SEPTEMBER 2005

Fakher Haider, our Iraqi fixer, is dead.

His body was found yesterday in the outskirts of Basra with his hands tied and a bag over his head. According to *The New York Times,* armed men wearing masks and claiming to be police officers abducted him from his home as his wife and children watched. A relative who viewed the body in the city morgue saw a bullet hole in his head and bruises on his back. Fakher had been reporting for *The Times* on friction among Basra's rival Shiite militias, which had— some said—infiltrated the police.

I call colleagues from the Iraq shoot. We remember Fakher and mourn among ourselves. *The NewsHour* and each of us individually contribute to a fund for the family. I read and reread articles about his death, and Fakher becomes

a vivid presence among my ghosts. At UC Berkeley one day, I disagree with an Al Jazeera producer about whether it is moral to risk the lives of fixers in our work. He says we must try to protect them but be willing to accept their deaths. Al Jazeera fixers have died on the job, he says. Getting important stories into the world is a worthy cause.

I say I don't believe I have the right to decide what story is worth another person's life.

The fixers and crews I've worked with over the years feel more precious to me than ever. Perhaps this is also a reflection of my age (sixty-two), but I doubt I'll ask others to accompany me again into potentially life-threatening situations.

TODAY, AT THE end of this exhumation, I have driven across the bay to Skywalker Ranch to visit Tik-tok again.

Pete Horner, audio mixer of *The Judge and the General,* is editing nearby on the Stanley Kubrick Stage, where we worked together eight years ago. His door is closed; the atrium is quiet. The ranch's Technical Building, a striking achievement of design and construction, feels almost sacred, like a church.

It was Tik-tok who led me back to the Oz stories after the apparition—myself as a little girl—asked, "What sent you on a path through death and destruction?" As before, he stands among tall plants in sunlight streaming from windows high above.

I step into the garden and touch him. He's made of hard plastic the color of copper. According to Pete, an acrobat who could bend almost in half animated him in Walter Murch's film *Return to Oz*.

Frank Baum made a motherless child, Dorothy Gale, the heroine of most of his books. Her parents had died, and she lived with a loving but joyless aunt and uncle on a farm in Kansas. He made the prairie parched, almost barren, as a symbol of Dorothy's mourning.

Baum understood that a young child who has lost a parent will search for what she has lost. This is especially true, I think, if the child isn't forewarned about a mother's or father's death, or if the foreverness of death is explained too late.

Using a tornado and other devices, Baum repeatedly lifts Dorothy from sadness into a beautiful, sometimes dangerous land, where she searches for the way home. She often helps others who are also looking for something missing in their lives. In the process, she makes friends and finds ways to be useful. In these travels, Baum gives Dorothy relief from self.

In places far from Kansas, I also found relief from self and sorrow by concentrating on the lives of others. I felt a kinship with the people I covered and especially with those who weren't told the truth about the disappearance of the people they'd lost.

I might have become a foreign correspondent anyway, but surely reporting from conflicted places was especially meaningful to me because of the early loss of my mother. Proximity to her suffering and death made me accept insecurity and also assertively embrace life, which I knew from experience to be fragile. Perhaps that's why, in this exhumation of mostly real experiences, I imagined myself with a white stallion in a train on the edge of disaster. My father and I did travel to California on the City of San Francisco after my mother died, and I searched for her at stops along the way. On the trip, I made friends with a girl from Tulip Lane in St. Louis. But we did not travel on the streamliner that got dangerously stranded in a historic blizzard in the Sierra Nevada. That happened in January 1952, the year before my mother died. When I first began imagining my father and me on that snowbound train, I was surprised but didn't resist. It felt like I was re-creating something that actually happened but was describable only through symbols. I needed the avalanche and the white stallion. Sky represents a force almost as powerful in my existence as death.

I nod my thanks to Tik-tok. He's shadowed now; the sun is moving west. It's time for me to stop living backward. I look at the little man one last time, walk out of the Technical Building, and drive back across to the bay to our home.

AFTERWORD

I RECOGNIZE THAT MEMORY and imagination are
closely linked, but I kept the latter under wraps when
writing about my work as a reporter and filmmaker. Those
memories have been checked with colleagues, notes, and
video. I did watch Ida Lupino in a mansion in Santa Barbara,
but I don't know what movie she was making. The lines of
dialogue come from *Jennifer*, which was released in 1953.

In later years, my father often apologized for not reveal-
ing that Mother was mortally ill. He said it was common in
those times to try to protect children from knowledge of a
parent's impending death.

No one has ever been arrested in Iraq for Fakher Haider's
murder. Matt Moyer, an American photographer, is producing a film about Fakher that will include tape from our
NewsHour shoot. I've seen photographs from the day when

Fakher saved Matt's life. They were covering an attack on prostitutes in Basra by vigilantes from a nearby mosque. An enraged man had aimed his AK-47 at Matt and seemed about to shoot. Fakher stepped between them and yelled, "We're journalists." The assailant hesitated and then turned and fired in another direction.

"If a drop of your blood spills, it is my blood spilling," Faker said.

A Drop of Blood is the title of Matt's film. I'm pleased that he and others, including the Committee to Protect Journalists, are increasingly recognizing and publicizing the courage and contributions of fixers in Iraq, Syria, Iran, Afghanistan, and other dangerous places. I am helping Matt Moyer in small ways with his film.

Judge Juan Guzmán was the first Chilean judge to indict Augusto Pinochet for murder. Pinochet's lawyers argued that he was mentally unfit to stand trial, but by early December 2006, high courts had ruled the former dictator competent. Pinochet was awaiting judgment on multiple counts of fraud, torture, and murder when he died on December 10, 2006.

CREDITS

Page 1: Part I

My father teaches me to ride a horse at the Darling Dude
Ranch in Alexandria, Minnesota. The image is a screenshot
from a home-movie shot by my uncle, William M. Mills Jr.,
and is reprinted courtesy of his children, my cousins. The
date must be about 1946.

Page 5

Photo of Tik-tok at Skywalker Ranch by Pete Horner.
Reprinted courtesy of Walter Murch, George W. Lucas,
John Null, and Pete Horner.

Page 13

Contact sheet of photos taken by Jaime Kibben in Cambodia
in April, 1993. Reprinted courtesy of Jeri Lynn Cohen.

Page 20

My mother and I stand together outside our house in Topeka
a few months after her first cancer operation in 1950. The
photo was taken by my father.

Page 33

John Knoop, Louis Saint-Lot, and I are walking together in
Port Au Prince, Haiti, in July 1994. The banner, which reads

"NON," represents the view of those opposed to the return of President Jean-Bertrand Aristide. Photo by Jaime Kibben is reprinted courtesy of Jeri Lynn Cohen.

Page 45

Salvador Allende and Pablo Neruda on stage in Santiago, Chile, during the largest pro-Allende rally of the 1970 election campaign. The screenshot is from the film, *Que Hacer* and is reprinted courtesy of Jim Becket.

Page 54

My father with me and my Toni doll—Christmas 1952. Photographer unknown.

Page 73

This is a composite by Mark Serr of two screenshots from *Thanh's War*, which was filmed in Binh Phu, Vietnam, in January 1990. A villager shows her wounds from an American bomb.

Page 81

The Union Pacific streamliner, City of San Francisco, January, 1952. Courtesy Union Pacific Railroad Museum, Council Bluffs, Iowa.

Page 85

Pham Thanh's family celebrates in Binh Phu, Vietnam, January, 1990. Photo by Jaime Kibben is reprinted courtesy of Jeri Lynn Cohen.

Pages 87-88

The John Balaban poem, "For the Missing in Action," comes from his book, *Words for my Daughter*, The National Poetry Series (Selected by W.S. Merwin), Copper Canyon Press, 1991, and is used courtesy of the author.

Page 99

This is a composite by Mark Serr of screenshots from *The Judge and the General*: Cecilia Castro Salvadores, Juan Carlos Rodriguez Araya, and their daughter Valentina, 1974; and (below) Judge Juan Guzmán, December 13, 2004, announcing his indictment of General Augusto Pinochet for murder.

Page 102

The stranded City of San Francisco, January 1952. Photograph courtesy of Ken Yeo.

Page 110

The upper part of this composite by Mark Serr is a screen-shot from *The Judge and the General* of the mother-of-pearl button, stuck in rust, on a rail brought up by a diver from Quintero Bay, Chile. During the dictatorship of General Augusto Pinochet, some political prisoners were tied to pieces of rail and dumped from helicopters into the bay. Below is a screenshot of a newspaper with a photo of Judge Guzmán on the day in September, 2004, when some rails were recovered. The headline reads, "Rails of Death."

Page 121

Composite by Mark Serr. The photo of the stranded City of San Francisco is reprinted courtesy of the Union Pacific Train Museum, Council Bluffs, Iowa.

Page 127: Part II

Louie, my teddy bear. Photo by Mark Serr.

Page 143

Photo by Scott Tong. Fakher Haider on a bridge over the Euphrates River in Nasariya, Iraq—May, 2003. Reprinted courtesy of Scott Tong.

ACKNOWLEDGMENTS

I AM DEEPLY GRATEFUL to Brenda Hillman, poet and friend, for encouraging me to write about the apparition of my younger self at Skywalker Ranch and then midwifing this book.

Special thanks also to editor Jack Shoemaker and his colleagues, Megan Fishman and Kelly Winton, at Counterpoint Press. They are virtuosos in their work.

Amy Rennert, a wise and resourceful agent, helped in many ways.

My husband, Chuck Farnsworth, novelist Linda Spalding (a fellow Topekan), Adam Hochschild, Arlie Hochschild, and Eve Pell critiqued several versions of the manuscript. As a journalist accustomed to working collaboratively, I also sought advice from Jim Lehrer, Michael Chabon, Douglas Foster, David Thomson, Deborah Gee, John Knoop, Ayelet

Waldman, Charles Spezzano, Elizabeth Law, John Balaban, and Robert Hass. Thank you to them and also to the editors of the literary journal *Brick*, who published excerpts from this work.

My sister, Marcia Anderson, supportive as always, provided photographs and keen insights.

Jeri Lynn Cohen graciously granted permission to use pictures taken by her husband, Jaime Kibben, who worked with me in Haiti, Cambodia, and Vietnam, among other countries. He also composed music for *Thanh's War*. Jaime was killed in an automobile accident in Israel in 2003

I learned about the 1952 three-day stranding of the City of San Francisco mainly from two sources: Robert L. Church's outstanding book, *Snowbound Streamliner* (Wilton CA: Signature Press, 2000), and articles in *The San Francisco Chronicle*. Reporters Art Hoppe and photographer Ken McLaughlin skied to the stuck train on January 15, 1952, and vividly described what they found. I read those articles at the library of the California State Railroad Museum in Sacramento, a mecca for train-lovers. I am grateful to librarians there and also to John J. Bromley, who, in 2009, answered many questions when I visited the Union Pacific Railroad Museum in Council Bluffs, Iowa. Ed and Barbara Czerwinski, residents of Truckee, California, and active volunteers with the Truckee Donner Railroad Society and the Truckee Donner Historical Society, read the manuscript for errors of railroad terminology. Any mistakes that remain are mine alone.